# Southeast Asia
*A Concise History*

Mary Somers Heidhues

# Southeast Asia
## *A Concise History*

with 131 illustrations and 11 maps

Thames & Hudson

Frontispiece: Bronze standing Buddha from Burma, dating
to the eleventh or twelfth century AD.

© 2000 Thames & Hudson Ltd, London

First published in hardcover in the United States of America in 2000 by
Thames & Hudson Inc., 500 Fifth Avenue, New York, New York 10110
thamesandhudsonusa.com

First paperback edition 2001

Library of Congress Catalog Card Number 99-66014
ISBN 0-500-28303-6

Printed and bound in Singapore by Kyodo Printing Co (S'pore) Pte Ltd.

# Contents

# Introduction

At first glance, Southeast Asia displays great variety and important divisions. A closer look reveals underlying similarities and significant unity. For while religion, history and politics have made the peoples and nations of Southeast Asia highly diverse, the region remains essentially united by location, climate and many common cultural traits.

Nearly all of Southeast Asia is tropical, hot and humid, as travellers to the region soon discover. Monsoonal winds alternate to bring dry and wet seasons each lasting half the year, the latter bringing heavy downpours. The changing winds facilitate seaborne trade and travel, too. There are exceptions: some mountain regions have cooler temperatures, for example, and northern Vietnam experiences rather chilly winters. Near the equator, monsoons are less pronounced and rain may fall during the entire year, something which made equatorial regions, with their dense vegetation, rather inimical to early settlement. This was the case in Sumatra and Borneo, for example, which even today are less populated than other areas of the Indonesian Archipelago. In eastern Indonesia, on the other hand, the dry season lasts so long that rice cultivation is often impractical and other crops such as sago (and in modern times, maize) are the dietary staples.

A useful, if not perfect, distinction is that between mainland and maritime Southeast Asia, the former part of the Asian continent, the latter stretching across island groups toward the Pacific Ocean and Australia. The mainland region includes the states of Vietnam, Cambodia, Laos, Thailand and Burma (Myanmar). The maritime region is composed of the Philippines, Indonesia, Malaysia, Singapore and Brunei Darussalam. Although West Malaysia, as a peninsula, is attached to the mainland, its religion, language and history clearly link it with neighbouring islands. Historically, mainland states generally controlled rice-growing agricultural populations and maritime states profited from seaborne trade. Buddhism is, broadly speaking, the majority religion on the mainland, while Islam dominates much of maritime Southeast Asia.

Rainfall and water have influenced lifestyles throughout the region. Great rivers flow through mainland Southeast Asia, most importantly the Irrawaddy and Salween in Burma, the Chaophraya in Thailand, the Red River in northern Vietnam, and the great system of the Mekong, rising in southern China and flowing all the way to the South China Sea. These are the traffic arteries of mainland Southeast Asia; the mountains that lie between them divide the land into discrete cultural areas with distinct languages such as Vietnamese, Khmer, Thai and Burmese.

The sea, by contrast, connects as much as it divides the separate islands of maritime Southeast Asia, enabling frequent and ready communication, aided by the seasonal winds. Thanks to this ease of contact, the cultures and languages of the Malayan Peninsula, the Indonesian Archipelago, and the Philippines are related, although minorities with distinct cultures do remain in the interior of some islands, just as they do in the mountainous areas of the mainland.

Heavy rainfall, combined with the control of water, also enables intensive irrigated rice cultivation, especially in lowland areas. Rice paddies cover a significant part of the landscape; rice – usually complemented by spicy side dishes – is the most important item in most Southeast Asians' diets.

Southeast Asians share other common cultural elements: most use kin terms for personal address, saying not 'you' but a word that assigns the speaker and the addressee to a place in a hierarchical relationship. One language, Javanese, carries the feeling for hierarchy even further, using different vocabularies to indicate the relative status of the speaker and the person spoken to.

Historically, women in Southeast Asia enjoyed much social freedom, owning property, participating in the marketplace, even reigning as queens – at least before stricter world religions like Islam and Christianity limited some of their activities. Southeast Asian kinship systems, too, give equal importance to relatives from the father's and the mother's side, in contrast to China, for example, with its strong emphasis on the male line.

History has introduced great diversity into Southeast Asia. The region has long been a crossroads for international trade, beginning in the first centuries after Christ with the traffic between its great neighbours, China and India. Indian influences in art, politics and religion reached much of Southeast Asia. The trade with China encouraged new economic developments and the formation of trading states; many Chinese immigrants later settled in the region.

All of the world's major religions have left their mark. (For a fuller discussion of Southeast Asian religions, see Chapter Three.) Theravada Buddhism is the dominant religion of mainland Southeast Asia. Many Vietnamese are Buddhists of the Mahayana tradition; their beliefs are also mixed with Taoist and Confucianist elements, while in the south of Vietnam Theravada Buddhism is also present. Islam is the dominant religion of the Malayan Peninsula and the Indonesian Archipelago. The Philippines are overwhelmingly Christian. The Indonesian island of Bali adheres to its own unique version of Hinduism. Upland minority groups still practice natural religions, though some have, over time, adopted the religion of the lowlanders or converted to Christianity. Despite the preponderance of the major religions, indigenous elements and earlier beliefs persist everywhere.

Southeast Asia's location exposed it to Western colonial penetration from the beginning of the sixteenth century. Portugal, Spain, the Netherlands, Britain, France and the USA all left their different impressions on Southeast Asian states. Most conspicuously, colonialism was responsible for today's national boundaries. These boundaries are often not historically or geographically determined, and may enclose peripheral ethnic groups living on both sides of the border.

The borders of colonial times kept Southeast Asia divided, and to an extent they still do. In recent years, however, the expansion of the Association of Southeast Asian Nations (ASEAN) beyond its original five founding members to include all states of the region has given Southeast Asia a framework for regional cooperation. ASEAN sponsors activities to bring together not just politicians, but scholars, businessmen, artists and professionals, encouraging a sense of regional identity. If the colonial powers defined the present boundaries of Southeast Asian states, political, cultural and economic dynamics now cross those boundaries and defy limitations.

INDIA

BANGLA-
DESH

CHINA

TAIWAN

BURMA (MYANMAR)

Irrawaddy

Red River

Hanoi

LAOS

Vientiane

Salween

Rangoon
(Yangon)

THAILAND

Chaophraya

Mekong

SOUTH
CHINA
SEA

Manila

Bangkok

Tonle Sap

VIETNAM

PHILIPPINE

ANDAMAN
SEA

GULF
OF
THAILAND

CAMBODIA

Phnom
Penh

CELEBE
SEA

Bandar Sri
Begawan

MALAYSIA

BRUNEI
DARUSSALAM

SABAH

Straits of Malacca

Kuala Lumpur

SINGAPORE

MALAYSIA

SARAWAK

SUMATRA

Kapuas

BORNEO
(KALIMANTAN)

SULAWESI

Musi

JAVA SEA

N

0          500 km

0          500 miles

Jakarta

INDONESIA

JAVA

SOUTHEAST ASIA TODAY

From north to south, ten very different countries make up contemporary Southeast Asia:

**Vietnam**, with its capital at Hanoi, had in 1997 a population of nearly sixty-six million. Under French colonial rule in the nineteenth century, the country was divided from north to south into three administrative units: Tonkin (Tonking), Annam and Cochin China. The overwhelming majority of the people are Vietnamese.

**Laos** has a comparatively small population of about five million. Its capital is Vientiane, and its population is Lao, although there are important minority groups.

**Cambodia**'s people are called Khmer; smaller minority groups and significant Vietnamese and Chinese minorities also live there. In 1975 the country was renamed Kampuchea (the Khmer pronunciation of Cambodia) but after the expulsion of the Khmer Rouge from the capital city Phnom Penh in 1978, the name Cambodia was restored. Its population numbers over eleven million.

**Thailand** was called Siam from its foundation in the thirteenth century until 1939, when the new name was adopted and its people, previously called Siamese, assumed the name Thai. 'Thailand' was an attempt to identify the land with the Tai peoples, who are a language group including the Thai/Siamese, but also

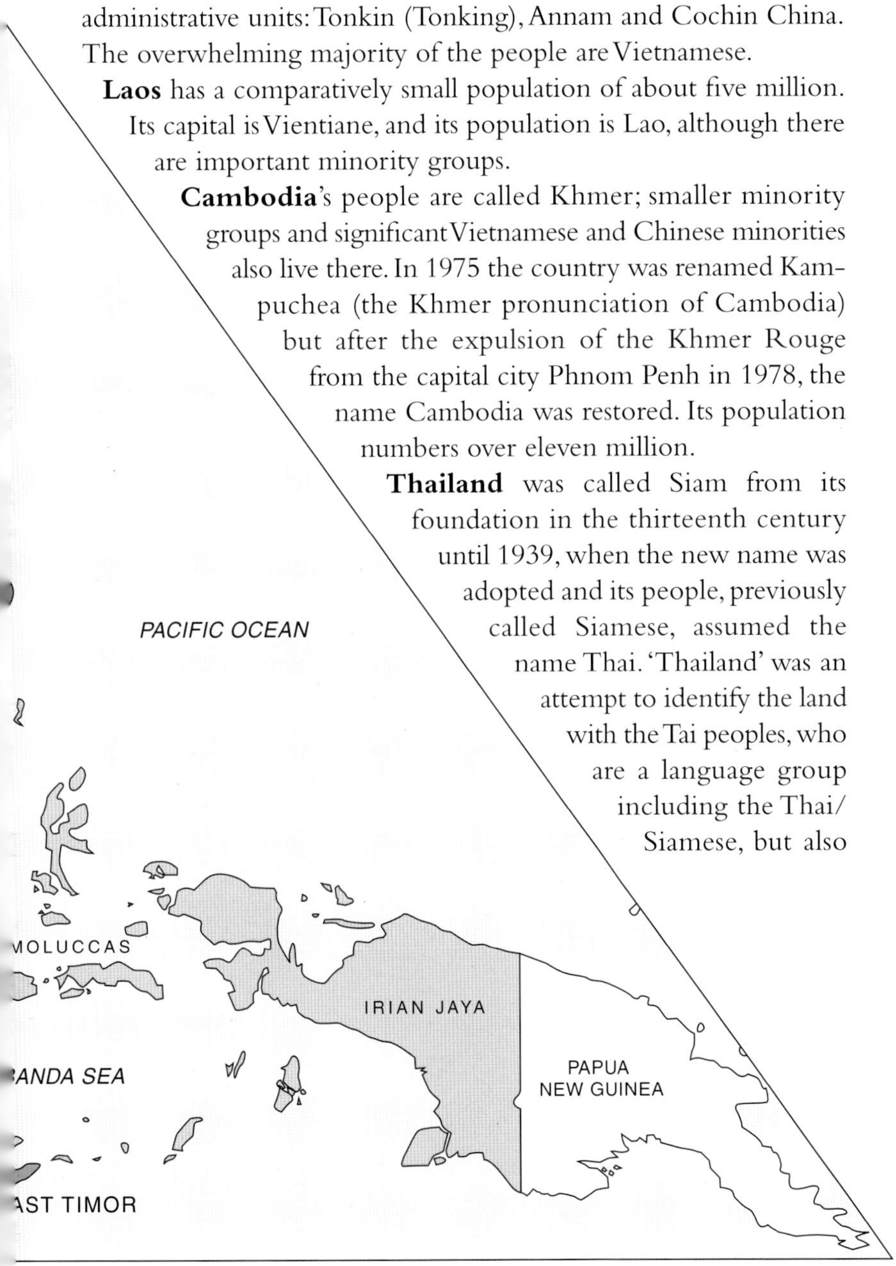

PACIFIC OCEAN

MOLUCCAS

IRIAN JAYA

BANDA SEA

PAPUA
NEW GUINEA

EAST TIMOR

the Lao, the Shan in Burma, and minorities in Vietnam and southern China. Thailand's capital is Bangkok. Its population of over sixty million includes a sizeable Chinese minority (perhaps eight per cent of the total population) as well as other groups.

**'Burma'** is an approximation of the Burmese name for the country. In 1988 the military leaders of Burma changed the name officially to Myanmar, a more correct transliteration of the same word. The capital, Rangoon, was also given its Burmese pronunciation, Yangon. The majority ethnic group are called Burmans or Myanmas. Citizens of Burma/Myanmar, who are not all Burmans, are usually called Burmese. Apart from small Indian and Chinese minorities, there are several million other Burmese who are not Burmans. The opposition leader Aung San Suu Kyi still calls her country Burma; many authors follow her example. The population in 1997 was nearly forty-four million.

**Indochina** is a geographic expression referring to the peninsula that includes the five mainland countries of Southeast Asia (Vietnam, Laos, Cambodia, Thailand and Burma), but usually excluding the Malayan Peninsula. French Indochina was the term adopted by the French for their Southeast Asian colonies, namely Laos, Cambodia and the three parts of Vietnam.

**The Philippines** take their name from the Spanish King Phillip II. They were a Spanish colony until 1898, when they were taken over by the United States of America. Although Filipinos celebrate their declaration of independence of that year, they only became fully independent in 1946. The population of about seventy-four million are from a number of ethnic groups, most of them related to Malays.

**Malaysia** has a western part, on the Malayan Peninsula, and an eastern part, in the north of the island of Borneo. The Malayan Peninsula, colonized by Britain, became independent in 1957 as the Federation of Malaya. Then, in 1963, the British colonies of Sarawak and Sabah (on the island of Borneo) and Singapore were added to Malaya, which became Malaysia. In 1965, Singapore left Malaysia, becoming independent. About sixty per cent of the population of nearly twenty-two million are Malays, while around twenty-five per cent are ethnic Chinese. Other minorities include those of South Asian origin and groups indigenous to Borneo. The capital is Kuala Lumpur.

**Singapore**, an independent republic since 1965, is a city-state with over three million inhabitants. Over seventy-five per cent of them are of Chinese origin; nearly all the rest are Malays or South Asians.

**Brunei Darussalam**, an Islamic sultanate that gave its name to the island of Borneo, has a population of just over three hundred thousand. Most of its inhabitants are Malays, but there is a Chinese minority of perhaps twenty per cent of the population. It was a British protectorate until 1984. The capital is Bandar Seri Begawan.

**Indonesia** declared independence in 1945. Four years later its sovereignty was finally recognized by the Netherlands. It covers the territory of the former Netherlands Indies or Dutch East Indies. Its capital, Jakarta, was called Batavia in Dutch colonial times. The largest country in Southeast Asia and one of the largest in the world, it has a population of over two hundred million, while its islands extend over an area comparable to that of Europe or the United States of America. Indonesians belong to many ethnic groups, the largest of which are Javanese, Sundanese, Balinese, Madurese, Minangkabaus and Bugis, though no group forms more than half of the population. Nearly all speak languages related to Malay, and the national language, *Bahasa Indonesia*, is practically identical to that of Malaysia, *Bahasa Malaysia* (modern Malay).

**East Timor**, a former Portuguese colony whose capital is Dili, was absorbed by Indonesia in 1975, but this annexation was not recognized, for example, by the European Union or the United Nations. In a plebiscite held in August 1999, its approximately eight hundred thousand inhabitants voted for independence, making them Southeast Asia's eleventh country. Following the vote, pro-Indonesian 'militia' groups rampaged through East Timor, killing and burning. The UN sponsored an international force to end bloodshed and secure the transition to independence.

SOUTHEAST ASIAN HISTORIES

Because the national units of Southeast Asia differ greatly in size, population density, wealth, form of government, religion, traditions, and in colonial experience, many histories of the area have concentrated on individual countries and not on common themes affecting the region as a whole. The novelty of the idea of Southeast Asia as a historical region is shown by D.G.E. Hall's *History of Southeast Asia*, which appeared as recently as 1955. Hall's was probably the first book to link the disparate experiences of the region in a single volume. Since then historians have confidently put aside the national approach and tried to view the area more broadly wherever possible. Volumes like the *Cambridge History of Southeast Asia*, edited by Nicholas Tarling, and the works of Anthony

Reid, especially *Southeast Asia in the Age of Commerce* (see the Short Bibliography on p. 186), have uncovered so many common features of the region that a strict nation-by-nation approach now seems inappropriate.

This text will proceed with a regional approach without ignoring the importance of individual national experiences. Although it aims to offer a general overview of Southeast Asian history, it cannot be overlooked that the author is especially interested in modern Indonesia. Hopefully this has not led to neglect of other areas. Finally, chapters deviate from a strict chronological order because themes persist and the past continues to live in the present. If the book serves its purpose, readers will want to learn more about the area. To this end, a list of readings follows at the end of the book.

NOTE ON SPELLINGS

Because this book is not for specialists, it does not use a specialized linguistic apparatus. Vietnamese and Sanskrit expressions are given without diacritical marks. Thai spellings follow those in Wyatt (1984). Indonesian-Malay terms are spelled according to the most recent orthography (in use since 1972), even if they refer to earlier persons or institutions (Sukarno not Soekarno; Masyumi not Masjumi). Readers should note that many Southeast Asians, including former presidents of Indonesia Sukarno and Suharto, have only one name, while it is common in many countries to refer to individuals by their first names.

For Chinese, Mandarin Pinyin transcription is used (in spite of the difficulties in pronunciation for the inexperienced), except in well-known expressions (for example Taoism).

Plurals are generally built with 's', even if that is not the case in the languages concerned. The text endeavours to limit foreign-language terms; a glossary of those that seemed unavoidable is appended.

## CHAPTER ONE

# Waterways
## *From Early Settlements to the First Maritime Kingdoms*

In prehistory, during times when glaciers bound surface water and the sea level fell, Borneo and the western islands of Indonesia (Java, Sumatra, Bali) were linked by a land bridge to the mainland, allowing humans – and flora and fauna – to cross easily. During warmer times, when sea levels rose, these islands were separated from the mainland of Asia. In time – perhaps thousands of years ago – islanders were such good sailors that the sea presented no barrier to their movement, and in historic times fishing, trade and seafaring were a major activity of maritime Southeast Asians, and an important one for mainlanders. Water and the management of water is vital to Southeast Asian cultures.

Remains of human habitation of Southeast Asia go back hundreds of thousands of years, but only in the last 4–5,000 years did the ancestors of most contemporary Southeast Asians reach the area, mixing with or dispersing earlier human settlers. Newcomers travelled to the Indochinese Peninsula along rivers rising in south and southwestern China or followed the shallow coastal waters around China; others crossed to Taiwan and from there migrated to the Philippines and beyond.

### EVIDENCE FROM PREHISTORY

The prehistory of Southeast Asia is still being discovered; controversies, suppositions and educated guesses prevail. Dense forest covered much of the region until this century. Without iron tools, early humans could not have felled the trees, and the jungle probably sustained only a few hunters and foragers with wild plants and animals. Where conditions were more hospitable, along the coasts and riverbanks, in caves or on alluvial plateaus where forests were more open (especially at times and in places of a generally drier climate), human settlements formed, at first using stone tools.

One group of settlements, found at several sites on the mainland, is named after Hoa Binh (Hoa Son Binh) Province in Vietnam, near Hanoi, where the first examples were found. The more sophisticated stone axes and knives of these Hoabinhian people enabled them to penetrate the edges of rainforests, where they lived mostly by hunting and gathering. The relics of these relatively mobile people, uncovered in caves or rock shelters, are dated at about 10,000 BC. Other early foragers probably lived along the sea coasts, but because the sea level has since risen, remains of their settlements lie submerged.

Both water and the humid tropical climate have destroyed many remains of early Southeast Asians. Even recently, these peoples lived in dwellings of bamboo, wood and thatch, and used implements and eating dishes made from equally perishable materials, leaving few traces for archaeologists. When writing did arise, it too was ephemeral. Most written texts were on strips of palm-leaves, which could disappear leaving little trace.

SOUTHEAST ASIANS

The movement of people has always played an important role in Southeast Asia, and continues to do so today. Scholars believe the ancestors of most present-day Southeast Asians were Southern Mongoloids who dispersed gradually through the region from the area of China south of the Yangtze River or from northern Southeast Asia. They began arriving at least 4,000 years ago. The China–Southeast Asia boundary is now a significant political divide, but in these early times southern China was culturally and environ-mentally a part of Southeast Asia. An expanding Chinese Empire only absorbed these southern regions into its culture and polity in the first millennium BC. Even today, some ethnic groups live on both sides of China's borders, linking Chinese with Southeast Asian peoples.

Only a few pockets of Negritos – in Thailand, West Malaysia and the Philippines – as well as the Melanesian people of New Guinea and its surrounding islands do not fit this type. Many eastern Indonesians also represent a mix of Melanesian and Southern Mongoloid traits; some preserve Melanesian languages.

There are two dominant language families in Southeast Asia, Austroasiatic and Austronesian. Linguists now believe that they ultimately developed from a single source somewhere within China. They were spoken by separate migrant groups that left southern China at about the same time, *c.* 4–5,000 years ago. Migrants to mainland Southeast Asia spoke languages of the Austroasiatic family. Today, representatives of this group include the languages of Cambodia (Khmer), Vietnam, parts of Burma and Thailand (the Mon minority), and small groups in Laos and in northeastern India. There is also a range of non-Austroasiatic languages spoken in mainland Southeast Asia; linguists usually assign these to the families Tai (spoken in Thailand, Laos and parts of neighbouring countries), Tibeto-Burman (spoken above all in Burma itself), and Miao-Yao (spoken by minorities in Thailand and Indochina). These were also introduced by migrants from southern China, though probably only in the last thousand years; all are spoken by ethnic minorities in southern China today.

A second group of migrants left China up to 5,000 years ago for Taiwan. These people spoke Austronesian languages and were capable seafarers. Their descendants moved on in small groups through the Philippines and toward Sulawesi, Borneo and the rest of maritime Southeast Asia, probably arriving in Java by about 1,000 BC. Archaeological evidence confirms this expansion. Identifiable pottery types, for example, are found at successive sites through the Philippines and southward toward Indonesia. Austronesian speakers eventually covered an enormous distance, spreading along an arc from Madagascar to Hawaii and New Zealand. Today the Austronesian language family includes, among others, Malayo-Polynesian languages such as modern Malay and Indonesian, Philippine languages, and Cham (spoken by a coastal people of the mainland who once dominated southern Vietnam). The languages of Taiwan's aboriginal people and some minority languages of the mainland are distant relatives.

### FARMING AND METALWORKING

The early migrants from China probably brought with them techniques of agriculture and especially rice cultivation that they developed further in the fertile landscapes of the Southeast Asian mainland. However, rice cultivation may have developed independently there: archaeological sites from 3–2,000 BC already show the domestication of rice and widespread use of pottery.

With agriculture, population density increased. Mainland sites, in particular on the Khorat Plateau of Thailand, where agricultural societies appeared by about 3,000 BC, show incipient efforts to control the water supply in order to ensure adequate rice harvests. With the later introduction of ironworking, settlements grew larger and agriculture more intensive. Animals like cattle and water buffalo were domesticated. Some of these settlements were surrounded by moats, possibly for defence, but the waterworks were connected to reservoirs and canals that may have been laid out to support rice cultivation.

Somewhere between 2,000 and 500 BC mainland peoples began using bronze and, centuries later, iron. Whether the working of bronze began independently in Southeast Asia, or whether it entered from China, is still a matter of debate. (The two metals, bronze and iron, appeared later and almost simultaneously in the Archipelago, in about 500 BC.) Trade and exchange increased and by 500 BC long-distance exchanges involved both China and India. Burial practices also became more elaborate; some sites give evidence of social differentiation in the greater quantity and quality of objects buried with the dead. The introduction of bronze in particular offered possibilities for distinguishing wealth and power, while iron allowed more effective weapons. In about 500 BC, small settlements began to agglomerate into larger units under their own chiefs.

Lamp-bearing kneeling figure from a tomb near Dong-son in northern Vietnam, dated to the fourth to second century BC. This bronze statue is a silent witness to the skills in metallurgy in Vietnam at this early period, when the famous Dongson drums were also made.

By far the most striking products of Southeast Asian bronze-working were the so-called Dongson or Heger Type I drums produced at Dong-son in Thanh Hoa province, northern Vietnam, from about 600 BC until as late as the third century AD. These magnificent metal drums, some of which are a metre high, may be based on forms that originally developed in Yunnan, but they themselves are uniquely Southeast Asian. Excavations have confirmed the extent and quality of bronze-working in Vietnam's Red River basin at that time. Expertly cast by the lost-wax method and weighing up to 100 kilograms (220 pounds), Dongson drums were both musical instruments and cult objects. Decorated with geometric patterns, scenes of daily life and warfare, animals and birds, and above all boats, drums became objects of trade and heirlooms. More than two hundred have been found throughout Southeast Asia as far as eastern Indonesia and even in southern China. This geographic dispersal may have taken place over centuries, as rulers traded or captured these prestigious items to add to their kingly regalia.

*(Above right)* The intricate geometric design of the face of a Dongson drum, with a sunburst at the centre surrounded by humans and birds. These impressive drums *(above)*, often part of a ruler's kingly regalia, were produced in northern Vietnam and have been found across a wide area of Southeast Asia. Some two hundred have been discovered. Other peoples, impressed by their beauty and and apparent spiritual power, produced similar artifacts with slightly different patterns.

These and other objects found far from where they were made confirm that trade and contact among Southeast Asian peoples was growing. In Java and Bali, bronze-working, which began later than on the mainland, brought a variety of artistic and useful objects by the first millennium AD, including bronze drums resembling those of Dongson but produced by a slightly different method. The megalithic remains on the Pasemah Plateau of South Sumatra, also dated to the first millennium AD, show a man carrying a Dongson drum. Nor was exchange limited to other Southeast Asian destinations: pottery found in north Bali shows that Indian goods reached that area two thousand years ago.

## EARLY STATES AND INDIAN INFLUENCES

Agriculture, trade, waterworks, early towns and social differentiation laid the foundation for the first Southeast Asian states. New crops, new artifacts and new concepts of kingship and rule followed trade, and the earliest maritime kingdoms arose.

When Europeans reached the region in the sixteenth century, few remains of the earliest states were visible, and even local people seemed to have forgotten them. This was especially true of maritime Southeast Asia, where climate and vegetation quickly reclaimed evidence of earlier human achievements. Only when scholars began to look at Chinese descriptions of the Southern Seas or Nanyang, the Chinese name for maritime Southeast Asia, did they uncover accounts of trading polities located there in the past. Monuments and stone inscriptions confirmed some of these accounts and archaeological investigations gradually found more evidence of the 'lost kingdoms', although the picture of them continues to change with new discoveries.

The most convincing account of the nature of these states is that proposed by the historian Oliver Wolters. He suggested that in the earliest Southeast Asian states power was based not on descent from an established lineage but on individual spiritual qualities. Wolters believes that the earliest Southeast Asian states arose when groups of small settlements coalesced around what he calls 'men of prowess', who were able to convince their followers of their superior spiritual resources. Neighbouring settlements might then recognize the dominant aura of such a man, allying themselves to him for

From the air, the geometric forms of the Borobudur resemble a mandala. Spiritual enlightenment increases as the believer moves up the square terraces and toward the stupa at the highest point, which is also its centre. Early Southeast Asian realms – in which power was concentrated in a strong centre surrounded by smaller satellite settlements – have also been described as mandalas.

protection or to add to their own status. When such a man of prowess died, his elevation to the status of honoured ancestor might provide unity over time for the group, and there are early monuments to such figures. Allied settlements formed a mandala, a spiritually powerful geometric figure, around the central settlement. The literal meaning of mandala is core (*manda*) and container or enclosing element (*-la*), but it can mean many things: in Buddhism and Hinduism, for example, it may be a geometric arrangement of deities in a holy place that creates a space within which the religious can meditate, protected from evil spirits. The configuration of the mandala may also be represented as a geopolitical alliance; such an ideal kingdom would exclude threats and undesirable influences. In the centre would be the ruler, surrounded by his officials, who themselves were at the centre of subordinate mandala formations.

If this was the basis of an early state, however, such constructions did remain inherently unstable. More easily observed is the cultural baggage of these rulers. Inscriptions and monuments throughout Southeast Asia, beginning in about AD 400, show the widespread adoption of Indian writing systems, of Hindu gods and goddesses, of Sanskrit vocabulary, especially in matters of religion and politics, and of Indian art forms. The ancestors began to be identified with Indian gods. This reception of Indian influences is all the more remarkable when it is realized that there was no known Indian colonization of the area: no Indian conquerors subjected Southeast Asian states, and only a few Indian traders settled in the area at the time.

Speculation about the origin of Indianization continues, but it seems that Southeast Asian traders first went to India perhaps as early as the second half of the second millennium BC. And it was Southeast Asian rulers who chose, in the first centuries of the Christian era, to adopt Sanskrit terms, Indian writing systems, and Hindu and sometimes Buddhist beliefs in order to increase their prestige and power. They imported Indian Brahmans and scribes to provide them with new knowledge, to create for them an illustrious ancestry, and to instruct in the ways of Siva (the most popular of the gods), Vishnu and Buddha. Religious devices, above all asceticism and meditation, were a way to increase the ruler's prowess and spiritual strength, and no doubt fitted well with indigenous traditions. Indianization was, for Southeast Asian rulers, a way to acquire power and legitimation. It served their purposes, not India's.

## FUNAN

As Southeast Asian trading polities grew, they made contact with China, and they soon sent tribute missions or trading delegations to the Chinese court. Imperial records of these missions enable historians to identify some early kingdoms. To China, these were emissaries from subordinate states, presenting their homage to the emperor of the civilized world. For Southeast Asians, in contrast, the missions not only offered an opportunity for trade at the Chinese capital, but they were a means of securing China's support for one or another ruler who wished to shore up his authority at home. In times of disorder or rivalry in Southeast Asia, missions were frequent; they became less so when reigns were stable and unchallenged.

The earliest Southeast Asian maritime trading polity mentioned by Chinese sources was called Funan. This was the Chinese name for a state of the third century AD, located in southern Vietnam and Cambodia. The Chinese observers assumed that it was a territorially organized state, though it may have been a loose association of several ports. Excavations at Oc-eo, near the present Vietnamese–Cambodian border, have confirmed the existence of an important settlement there, contemporary with Chinese reports. Archaeologists have found evidence of canals linking this inland site to the Gulf of Thailand. They believe that the settlement at Oc-eo acted as an entrepôt for the trade between China and India from the second to sixth centuries.

Because early seagoing traders hugged the coastline, Oc-eo occupied a strategic location at the bend of the Indochinese Peninsula.

An early image of the widely venerated Hindu god Siva, from the ninth-century Bakong temple in Hariharalaya, not far from Angkor. Many early Southeast Asian rulers identified with Siva, often in combination with devotion to other Hindu gods or to Buddhism, as well as to pre-Hindu practices.

This tin disk is a Roman coin found at the site of Oc-eo, near the coast of the Gulf of Thailand. Scholars believe Oc-eo was a significant trading centre and may have been part of the political entity the Chinese called Funan.

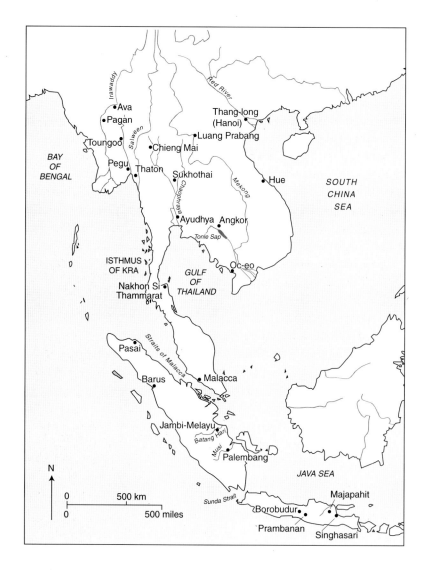

It was far enough inland to provide a sheltered harbour, while its neighbourhood produced enough rice to provision visitors. It also lay on the Maritime Silk Road, a route linking China with India, the Near East, and, at the western extreme, Rome. This sea route did not round the Malayan Peninsula in this period, but rather crossed it by land at the Isthmus of Kra, now in southern Thailand. By offering an alternative to the traditional land-based Silk Road through Central Asia, especially when unrest there interrupted overland communications, it contributed directly to the nascence of the first Southeast Asian trading polities. Funan's tribute gifts to the Chinese emperor show how sturdy its sailing vessels were: once it sent elephants, another time a rhinoceros.

## CHAMPA

The trading polity of Funan used to be seen as a predecessor of modern Cambodia, but more recent writing identifies it as a fore-runner of Champa, which ruled in what is now southern Vietnam until the seventeenth century. The Khmers, who succeeded to rule what is now Cambodia, were not a maritime people as the Chams were, but lived further inland (the name 'Khmer' means 'forest-dweller'). Chinese sources only use the name Champa in the eighth century, however, so the connection between Funan and Champa remains hypothetical.

The maritime kingdom of Champa fell prey to Vietnamese and Khmer expansion. Its most important relics are at My Son in southern Vietnam and, like this temple, show strong Indian influence. There is still a Cham minority, now predominantly Muslim, in southern Vietnam.

The Cham people belong to the group of Austronesian speakers, in common with much of island Southeast Asia. Scholars have come to believe that Champa, which was strongly influenced by Indian religion and art, was a group of island-like settlements separated from one another by mountains, but open to the sea to the east. Conse-quently, despite being on the mainland, it had more in common with maritime or 'archipelagic' polities. Among its separate communities, with their semi-nomadic seafaring populations, different centres established hegemony over certain areas at different times. In addition, they organized trade and exports somewhat in the way of later maritime kingdoms, exchanging goods with the mountain ethnic groups and perhaps integrating them into their state organization.

Chams today are Hindu or Muslim (the latter confirming their relationship to Malays) and during the period of French colonization, officials often referred to them as 'Malays'. Their history is still largely unwritten and their relations with other Malay states little explored, but it seems reasonable to include Champa among the early maritime states under Indian cultural influence and in exchange with China.

## SRIVIJAYA

Malay sailors from the Indonesian Archipelago visited Funan. They introduced their own products for sale in foreign markets: aromatic resins from the tropical forest (a substitute for frankincense and myrrh from the Near East), camphor, sandalwood, and spices like nutmeg and cloves. Both India and China welcomed these products, and Malays began visiting ports there, too. Chinese sources noted that Southeast Asian ships could bring tons of cargo from southern China to India swiftly. Thus it was a logical step to bypass the Indochinese Peninsula (and Funan) and direct the Asian entrepôt trade to the Archipelago itself and through the Straits of Malacca, especially since more and more long-distance commerce was being carried in Malay vessels, in part thanks to better sailing techniques. In addition, Buddhism had gained influence in India. Being a missionizing religion, which Hinduism was not, Buddhism conceivably now encouraged Indian travel abroad.

The result was that by the sixth century the Maritime Silk Road had shifted. Most ships trading internationally had begun to sail through the Straits of Malacca instead of sending their goods across the Isthmus of Kra. Funan and its neighbours were soon eclipsed by the Sumatran kingdom of Srivijaya at sea and by early Khmer states on land.

Srivijaya was at first known to historians only from Chinese accounts. Then in the nineteenth and twentieth centuries a number of stone inscriptions written in old Malay with Sanskrit borrowings and in an Indian script were found around Palembang in South Sumatra, in neighbouring islands, and as far away as modern Nakhon Si Thammarat in Thailand. These inscriptions, dating from the seventh to eighth centuries, permitted scholars (in particular George Coedès) to confirm the existence of Srivijaya, to name some of Srivijaya's rulers, and even to describe something of its internal organization. Until recently, archaeological evidence for Srivijaya was so sparse that some historians doubted whether its centre was indeed, as others insisted, in South Sumatra. Today, the evidence for the South Sumatran port of Palembang as first capital – though not the only capital – of Srivijaya is overwhelming. Recent excavations at Palembang have uncovered large quantities of Chinese porcelain of the Tang Dynasty (seventh to ninth centuries), a number of

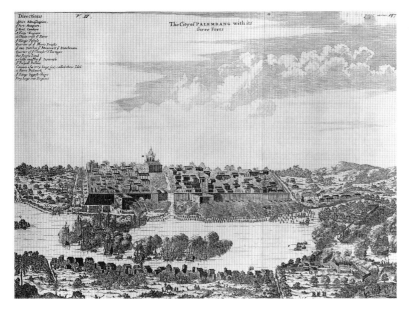

A seventeenth-century view of Palembang, former capital of Srivijaya and by then a Dutch trading post. Prominent is the wide Musi River, which even now permits ocean-going ships to reach the city and its harbour. The ruler of Srivijaya is said to have thrown gold bricks as an offering of thanks into the river, the source of his wealth.

large Buddhas and a magnificent statue of the Hindu elephant god Ganesha, dated to the tenth century.

Srivijaya was, above all, a trading polity. The alternating monsoon winds meant that a sailing ship could not travel from China to Southeast Asia and on to India in an uninterrupted voyage. Long-distance traders had to wait in a Southeast Asian harbour for up to five months until the winds changed and they could carry their cargo to its ultimate destination. Such a port had to offer security from pirates and storms, and have access to food and water to provision the traders. Like Funan, Srivijaya had both security and supplies. In the seventh century Palembang was closer to the coast than it is today and the Musi River, on which it lies, offered a convenient and sheltered harbour. Srivijaya's rulers understood their statecraft well, using mobile boat-dwelling people like the *orang laut* (sometimes called sea nomads) to police the Straits of Malacca, repelling pirates, directing traders (who might think of going elsewhere) to the Srivijayan port, and enforcing their hegemony over rival harbours.

The rulers also maintained an army recruited from their subjects. In the late seventh century, the king himself led his forces to attack the nearest rival port, Jambi, also on Sumatra and then called Melayu (probably the origin of the word Malay), setting the stage for Palembang's hegemony. Finally, although South Sumatra is not a rich rice-producing area, the lowlands along the Musi near Palembang grew some rice, while more may have been brought from upriver areas and perhaps even from neighbouring Java to feed the visitors.

Apart from political and ecological factors, religion contributed to Srivijaya's dominance. A devout seventh-century Chinese Buddhist, I Ching, travelling on pilgrimage to India, stayed for years in Srivijaya and left a record of his experiences there. He described the king as a patron of Buddhism and the town as an important centre of Buddhist studies:

'In the fortified city of Fo-shih [Palembang], there are more than a thousand Buddhist priests whose minds are bent on study and good works.... If a Chinese priest wishes to go to the west to understand and read [the original Buddhist texts] there, he would be wise to spend a year or two in Fo-shih and practice the proper rules there; he might then go on to central India.'

Like Funan, Srivijaya was not a territorial state. Its political organization is best described by the image of the mandala, the formation that concentrates power. Within the realm were several centres of power of differing importance. The task of the ruler was to maintain them in a relationship of subordination to his person and to ensure that none broke off and became the centre of a rival mandala. For this purpose Srivijaya had a corps of officials, whose titles are known from inscriptions.

The king ruled the port city personally with his staff. Most officials had Sanskrit titles, though the shippers had a Malay title – further evidence that the Malays were the dominant group in transportation, even when the merchants themselves came from China or India. The officials ruling other ports were more like headmen than employees of the king. Nonetheless, Srivijaya's powerful navy of *orang laut* bound them together and, probably, ensured a monopoly of the trade in valuable commodities like camphor from Barus in northwest Sumatra, something highly prized in China.

The loose bonds that connected the various parts of the mandala left the kingdom somewhat unstable. A king needed political intelligence to maintain his authority against challengers in the capital, but more importantly he needed to treat lesser rulers within his sphere with the classical tools of diplomacy: cajolery, threat and reward. Foreign trade provided the king with valuable items like textiles, porcelain and perhaps bronze drums with which he could reward a loyal entourage and subordinate rulers.

Above all, the king needed to prove his superior spiritual endowments. Srivijaya's rulers successfully blended symbols from Malay traditions, Buddhism and Hinduism to underline their powers. The importance of seaborne trade to their realm is indicated in Arab accounts from the ninth and tenth centuries of a daily ceremony in which the ruler threw a brick of gold into the sea, proclaiming, 'Look, there lies my treasure.' He was also 'lord of the mountains', the second pole of his power, where the upstream people who provided him with valuable natural products resided.

The inscribed stones that show the extent of Srivijaya's authority also show the threats of earthly force or supernatural retribution that kept more distant polities in line. Some of the stones, in the shape of male and female sexual organs, the *linga* and *yoni*, were oath-taking stones: water was poured over the stone and drunk to underline the efficacy of sworn loyalty. The inscriptions promised rewards to the faithful and retribution to those who dishonoured the oath. One of these, the Telaga Batu stone from Sabukingking, near Palembang, is crowned by a seven-headed *naga* (snake), a symbol of water (Srivijaya's element) and fertility. Oath-takers would read:

Om! Success!…All of you, as many as you are – sons of kings,…chiefs, army commanders, confidants of the king, judges, surveyors of groups of workmen, surveyors of low castes, cutlers, clerks, sculptors, naval captains, merchants,…and you – washermen of the king and slaves of the king – all of you will be killed by the curse of this imprecation; if you are not faithful to me, you will be killed by the curse….

However, if you are submissive, faithful and straight to me and do not commit these crimes….You will not be swallowed with your children and wives…. Eternal peace will be the fruit produced by this curse which is drunk by you….

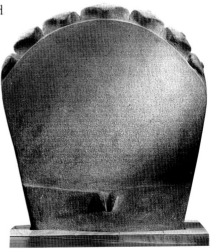

The seventh-century Telaga Batu stone, Srivijaya's longest known inscription, found near Palembang. Nearly one and a half metres (five feet) high, it lists officials of the realm and displays an oath of loyalty to the ruler. Seven cobra heads give it an ominous appearance. Water poured over the stone was collected through the *yoni* (vagina) at the base and drunk with the oath.

The furthest reaches of Srivijaya's authority were to allied kingdoms that accepted Srivijaya's regulation of trade but maintained their independence. This would have been true of the settlement where the Nakhon Si Thammarat inscriptions were found, for these were not linked to oaths of loyalty, and, perhaps, of central Java, which was allied with Srivijaya.

Srivijaya's power endured from the seventh to tenth centuries. In 1025 seamen based in the Chola realm in southern India raided Palembang. Srivijaya survived, but it never recovered its glory. Before the end of the eleventh century, its centre seems to have moved to the nearby port of Jambi-Melayu on the Batang Hari River. Palembang continued to trade with China, but not under the name of Srivijaya.

The move to Jambi-Melayu could not restore Srivijaya's power. Rivals were also gaining ground in Java and trade routes were shifting further east. In the late thirteenth century, the kingdom fell prey to the Tai (see p. 60), who acquired hegemony over some of its dominions on the Malayan Peninsula. In 1260, Jambi-Melayu succumbed to an attack from Java, which seems to have established its hegemony over the kingdom. Gradually, this polity turned its attention inward, away from the sea, and authority over Jambi-Melayu passed to the upland kingdom of Minangkabau, whose fourteenth-century ruler, Adityavarman, may be considered the last king of Srivijaya. He may have been the son of a Malay princess of Srivijaya and a Javanese prince. Sent to Sumatra, he threw off Javanese hegemony and established himself as an independent ruler in the uplands.

This ruler's religion, and his statecraft, were strongly shaped by the esoteric Tantric school of Buddhism, which had been influential in Palembang and also in Java. A four-metre-high statue, representing Adityavarman as Bhairava, the demonic incarnation of the god Siva, was unearthed in the uplands of Jambi-Melayu, on the border of Minangkabau territory, in 1906. The king stands above a wreath of human skulls, holding a skull in his hand, a tiny Buddha figure in his hair – an example of Southeast Asian syncretism, combining Siva and Buddha, that Adityavarman may have learned in eastern Java. A related inscription hints at the practice of human sacrifice. Extensive remains of Tantrist shrines are located nearby.

Srivijaya's culture followed its political influence. It patronized Buddhism and spread the Malay language, making it the dominant language not only of much of Sumatra, but of the Malayan Peninsula. Historians believe Srivijaya laid the foundation for the use of Malay as a *lingua franca* in the entire Archipelago, and as the national language of Malaysia, Indonesia, Brunei and Singapore today.

Although Srivijaya's mantle seems to have passed to Jambi-Melayu after 1025, many trading settlements soon grew up in Sumatra. Changes in trading patterns in China under the Song Dynasty, which itself was under pressure from the Mongol invaders from the north, led some Chinese traders to establish more permanent bases in Southeast Asia. Among these was Kota Cina (Chinese Town) on Sumatra, not far from the modern city of Medan on the Straits of Malacca. Excavations have revealed a large urban site, a centre of trade and crafts, that existed until the fourteenth century, possibly surrounded – as were Chinese settlements but not Southeast Asian ones – by a wall. That its name, Kota Cina, is still used today confirms the part played by Chinese immigrant traders in earliest urbanization, a role they would continue in later centuries.

Srivijaya's inheritance finally passed in the fifteenth century to the port of Malacca (Melaka) on the Malayan Peninsula. With some Chinese support – given that China was again interested in securing peaceful trade through the Straits – Malacca took up Srivijaya's role as entrepôt. Malacca's genealogy traces the ancestry of its first ruler to a kingdom near Palembang, without mentioning the name Srivijaya. This port polity, whose rulers soon converted to Islam and took the title of sultan, also utilized the *orang laut* to enforce its hegemony in the area. Like Palembang, Malacca provided a haven for foreigners waiting for the changing winds before they could sail onward. With its codes of law and the prestige that its court and culture came to acquire, Malacca set an example for all future Malay Islamic sultanates in the region.

## WATERWAYS, SETTLEMENTS AND TRADE

The image of Srivijaya's monarch feeding gold bricks to the sea underscores the vital importance of the sea, the rivers and the flows of water to all of Southeast Asia. Srivijaya's power was based on trade and on waterways, and boats and water transport were essential to all coastal, insular and riverine peoples of the region. People and ideas diffused along the river routes of the mainland. In maritime Southeast Asia, the short distance between islands facilitated cultural interchange. The French historian Denys Lombard spoke of the sea not as a barrier but as a link, a hyphen (*la mer comme trait d'union*), while the large rivers were essential paths of communication and cultural contact. On the great island of Borneo, rivers carried almost all traffic until quite recently, as they did in many other parts

*(Opposite)* The fourteenth-century Srivijayan king Adityavarman represented as Bhairava, Siva in his demonic aspect. Influenced by Tantrism, this four-metre (thirteen-feet) high figure stands on a pedestal of skulls, holding a skull and a knife in its hands. It was discovered in the Minangkabau highlands above Jambi-Melayu.

of the region, for example along the Mekong River. Land travel was arduous or impossible until colonialism and development brought roads. Even now rivers are major communication routes.

Boats and ships were and are a vital part of Southeast Asian life. Historically, some made use of outriggers to add stability, as do Polynesian vessels today. Apart from their practical uses for fishing and transportation, they continue to link peoples with their real and mythical past. Boat names often appear in names of settlements in insular Southeast Asia, and traditions tell how founders arrived in ships. The great Dongson drums reached their destinations far from Vietnam by boat. The ship is an important feature of traditional art. Boats are depicted on the Dongson drums, in the design of houses whose roofs resemble the prows of ships, and they are woven into the designs of textiles like the ship cloths of Lampung in south Sumatra.

The Malay *orang laut* still maintain a lifestyle oriented to the sea, and some of them even now live most of their lives on their boats. In more recent times, Chinese and then Western ships took over Southeast Asia's long-distance shipping. For inter-island traffic however, the Bugis of South Sulawesi carry an important share of goods from port to port in their all-wooden vessels, and they may well be today's successors to the intrepid Malay seamen of Srivijaya.

A Jakarta dockworker against the background of the wooden Bugis sailing vessels that still ply the waters of the Archipelago. The Bugis, from the island of Sulawesi, follow in the long tradition of Malay seafarers.

Traditional Toba Batak houses in northern Sumatra have, like many in the Indonesian Archipelago, peaked roofs resembling the prows of ships – a reminder, it is said, of these land-dwellers' arrival in the islands by boat, many centuries ago.

Many Southeast Asians live along rivers – even over them – or on ground that floods regularly, such as the Cambodian countryside *(below)*. Houses raised on stilts offer easy access to the water. Even on higher ground, houses are often elevated; this makes them easier to ventilate and offers animals a shady refuge below. Vietnamese and Javanese, however, build at ground level.

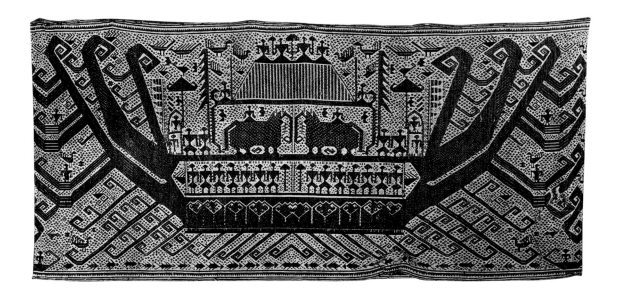

Ceremonial 'ship cloths' from Lampung, Sumatra, also depict boats. This vessel carries two elephants, as well as a number of human passengers and crew.

A modern successor to Srivijaya and Malacca, a port-polity and not a territorial state, still provides a centre for international trade in the Straits of Malacca. Since it was founded in 1819, Singapore has grown to become the entrepôt for Asia's trade with the world. It is a very different polity from Srivijaya, but nevertheless one that continues its most important international role of gathering products from the hinterland of Malaysia and Indonesia for sale to the world, and acting as an intermediary for Asian and world commerce.

## CHAPTER TWO

# Temples and Rice
## *Land-Based Kingdoms*

In the lowland regions of mainland Southeast Asia and on the fertile, volcanic island of Java kingdoms arose at least as early as the fifth century AD that were based on the growing of rice, especially wet rice, a technique that enables a relatively large population to survive on relatively little land. Elaborating their agricultural techniques through control of water, artificial irrigation, and other means of intensification, these kingdoms laid the foundation for major land-based states in which trade and international contact were usually of only secondary interest.

Wet-rice agriculture requires large inputs of labour compared to rotating dry field or swidden (slash-and-burn) practices, the second major form of rice agriculture in Southeast Asia. Swidden agriculture is practised in less densely settled areas where labour is at a premium and where ample land, often of low fertility, is available for exploitation. Although some scholars suggest that wet-rice cultivation is very ancient in Southeast Asia, even that it originated there, most believe that the technique arrived with early migrants from China and that swidden practices are the older ones; they are now more typical of semi-migrant upland minority peoples. Wet-rice agriculture, on the other hand, binds a population to fields and to irrigation systems. Control of people becomes as important as control of land. Furthermore, whether using natural rainfall or artificial irrigation, it produces surpluses that allow many people to engage in non-agricultural pursuits: government, religion, handicrafts or art, all useful to early land-based kingdoms. Although rice agriculture remained the most important activity, many crafts and trades flourished in these societies. Weaving and pottery were usually the domain of women, metal-working that of men. In Java, village markets met every five days, while a refined system brought local products to larger markets and to coastal harbours.

## SOUTHEAST ASIAN KINGSHIP

Like maritime states such as Srivijaya, land-based kingdoms drew subordinate states into their spheres, creating what have been variously described as 'galactic polities', 'concentric realms' or 'mandalas' (see pp. 21–22). Subordinate polities had their own centres, and they might break off and join other centres or form their own, making these states similarly unstable. Unlike modern nation-states, Southeast Asian kingdoms thought boundaries unimportant. Control of the centre was their paramount concern; the capital stood for the entire realm.

Much of the instability of early Southeast Asian realms resulted from internal factors. Important was the lack of fixed rules for royal succession. The title of crown prince was little known, and where it did exist the position immediately made its holder a rival not only to the king himself but to any number of other potential successors. These were numerous because any male closely related to the king – son, brother, uncle, cousin – might have a claim to succeed him. Since most rulers had a number of wives and concubines, their relatives were legion. A woman might also succeed, either in her own name or that of her son or husband, or she might bring in her own family as competitors to the royal line. The female line could be as prestigious as the male. Huge palace complexes might harbour hosts of scheming relatives; poisoning, murder and treachery were by no means unknown at the centre of power.

Another contributor to instability were the great migrations from the mainland of Burmans, Tai or other peoples entering Southeast Asia from southern China. After the Mongol (Yuan Dynasty) invasions of the thirteenth century and the defeat of Pagan in northern Burma, a Tai people, the Shan, established a successor kingdom there. The southern expansion of the Vietnamese from the eleventh to eighteenth centuries entirely displaced the realm of Champa and weakened Cambodia.

## KINGSHIP AND DISPLAY

The great importance of the centre is reflected in ancient capitals by their orientation to the cardinal points, a pattern repeated in palaces, temples and monuments. Control of the realm radiated from the centre, the capital, and within the capital, from the palace. A capital or a temple complex might be so built that it represented the kingdom itself. Within the palace, the throne and the kingly regalia – including dagger, sword or kris, umbrella, spear and even elephants – were the real locus of power. A rival might dethrone a monarch simply by seizing his regalia.

Underpinning political control was a plenitude of ritual and display, so much so that Clifford Geertz described Southeast Asian statecraft – in this case as practised in petty kingdoms on Bali – as 'theatre state'. Appearance reflected, but also created, reality. This description by an early Chinese visitor records the Cambodian ruler's love of display:

Every three days the King goes solemnly to the audience-hall and sits on a bed made of five pieces of sandalwood and ornamented with seven kinds of precious stones. Above this bed is a pavilion of magnificent cloth, whose columns are of inlaid wood. The walls are ivory, mixed with flowers of gold. The ensemble of this bed and the pavilion form a sort of little palace, at the background of which is suspended…a disc with rays of gold in the form of flames. A golden incense burner, which two men handle, is placed in front…. More than a thousand guards dressed with cuirasses and armed with lances are ranged at the foot of the steps of the throne, in the halls of the palace, at the doors and peristyle.

In the fourteenth century King Hayam Wuruk of Majapahit on Java went to visit his people:

When the King set out…the royal servants attended him in great numbers, And the whole breadth of the royal highway was filled with a limitless number of laden carriages standing like a solid wall.
Man on man, footman on footman they came with ox-carts before and behind,
While other followers went on foot, crowded, confused and jostling, with elephants, horses and so on in vast numbers.
…the carriage of the King, adorned with gold and flowing jewels;
Its appearance was different: it was a palanquin with screens, with gleaming lac, broad, and its brightness shining roundabout, dazzling.

Since a kingdom was defined by its centre, relations with more distant, peripheral groups were fluid. Ideally they were satellites, providing political tribute and participating in an exchange of valued upland and forest products for rice, salt and, where trade permitted, imports from abroad. In some cases, such as Angkor and Majapahit, the centre was strong enough to actually govern subordinate regions through a centrally directed bureaucracy.

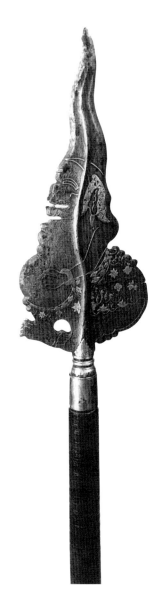

A ceremonial spear might be part of the royal regalia that bestowed legitimacy. This example bears an effigy of Semar, the widely known and loved clown-deity from the *wayang* shadow-puppet theatre.

The twentieth-century Cambodian king S.M. Monivong is carried to his coronation on a palanquin, shaded by a golden umbrella – another item of kingly regalia – and attended by members of his court.

Kings often titled themselves *chakravartin*: universal monarch or, literally, 'he who turns the wheel of the universe'. Statecraft meant convincing subordinate rulers to accept a king as their overlord. Since this involved primarily ceremonial recognition, such alliances remained fragile and in practice new chakravartins might emerge.

Between the eighth and the fourteenth centuries, land-based realms created the great monuments for which Southeast Asia is justly famous, including those of Angkor, Borobudur, Prambanan and Pagan. These religious and, to a lesser extent, political edifices are preserved in stone or brick; their wooden predecessors are lost. There are also innumerable inscriptions on stone, gold or copper, as well as statuary and literary texts to confirm the glory of these kingdoms, and historians can tell much about the practices at court. Unfortunately, the records and implements of daily life in these realms remained as perishable as those of maritime peoples, although some visual depictions are found in temple reliefs.

## ANGKOR AND CAMBODIA

Funan had continued to send trade and tribute missions to China until the sixth century. Some time later, Chinese annalists noted that Funan had been replaced by Zhenla (the Chinese writing system, relying on fixed syllables, gives only a hint of what the name may have been). This new polity (or polities), composed of ethnic Khmers (Cambodians), had its centre in dry, relatively infertile plains on the lower Mekong River, near that natural reservoir of the Mekong, the Tonle Sap or Great Lake. During the monsoon, rainwater, augmented by melting snow from Tibet where the river rises, gushes into the lower reaches of the Mekong with such force that its tributary stream, the river of the Tonle Sap, actually reverses direction and empties its contents into the Great Lake. The lake increases in size from 2,700 square kilometres (1,040 square miles) to a maximum of 10,000 (3,900). When the waters begin to recede in October, the deposit of silt fertilizes the fields, and the lake and its ponds deliver a rich harvest of fish. Like maritime Southeast Asia, but in a very different way, this rice-based economy profited from its relation to water.

Scholars are uncertain to what extent Zhenla was a single kingdom or a collection of statelets. Its king Jayavarman II, who reigned from the late eighth century to about 834, is said in later inscriptions to have freed the land from the rule of 'Java' (perhaps not meaning the island of that name), subdued smaller principalities, and unified the realm. By about this time, artificial irrigation of rice had become widespread. Jayavarman II finally established his capital north of the Great Lake, settling at Hariharalaya (modern Roulos), close to Angkor. The city's name derived from Harihara, a god or image that combines the attributes of the Hindu gods Siva and Vishnu. In 802 Jayavarman II was enthroned as a *dewaraja*, a god-king, probably meaning that he identified his person with the Hindu god Siva. After his reign there is a silence of half a century, perhaps indicating a return of internal division, but the foundations now existed for one of Southeast Asia's most durable kingdoms.

Between the ninth and thirteenth centuries, successive Khmer rulers (though not necessarily direct successors), their priests, monks, craftsmen, artists and labourers constructed Angkor. Little remains of the city, and even the residences of kings and monks are largely lost, but the temples were of stone and brick, their ornamentation of stone and bronze, and they have endured. Angkor was erected at a beautiful location by generations of builders, who embellished the site with temples, monasteries, residences, walkways and reservoirs. Immense pools of water express the importance of waterworks to the society. Holding water for irrigation, but also reflecting the sky and the man-made surroundings, they enhance the aesthetic impression.

Because it was constructed over several centuries, Angkor incorporates different artistic styles. Angkor's founder, King Yasovarman (r. 889–c. 910), moved his capital from Hariharalaya to a site north of the Great Lake. His first temple, Phnom Bakheng, was constructed on a hill and was itself a representation of a mountain, Mount Meru, the centre of the Hindu and Buddhist universe and the magical centre of his kingdom. Within the Phnom Bakheng was a linga, a phallic symbol and sign of Siva, but also a symbol of the king himself. He built monasteries and waterworks, and certainly erected other edifices that have since disappeared. The name Angkor (from the Sanskrit *negara*, meaning both capital city and state) signifies both the realm and the temple and urban complex.

Subsequent kings added to the complex, which is often erroneously named Angkor Wat. In fact Angkor Wat is its largest monument (*wat* means temple), 60 metres (200 feet) high and built by Suryavarman II (r. 1113–c. 1145) in the twelfth century to honour and associate with Vishnu and to celebrate the reunification of the kingdom after a time of strife. While the temple itself represents both the kingdom and the universe, its bas-reliefs show episodes from

Angkor Wat, built in the twelfth century, is the largest temple in Angkor; here its beauty is enhanced by reflection in one of the site's reservoirs. It was built by King Suryavarman II, who dedicated it to Vishnu. Angkor Wat is also a calendar: the sun rises precisely over its main tower on the first day of the Indian solar year.

the life of Rama, an incarnation of Vishnu, as related in the Indian epic *Ramayana*; scenes from another Indian epic, *Mahabhrata*; and some 'historical' court scenes. Angkor Wat may be Suryavarman II's tomb, but it is also an observatory: the sun rises directly over the temple on the day of the summer solstice, the beginning of the solar year in the Indian calendar. Its dimensions reflect Indian notions about time. Beautiful as it is, in its day Angkor Wat was even more impressive, its towers gilded and its exterior painted white.

In the nineteenth century, a visitor wrote of Angkor Wat:

At the sight of this temple, one feels one's spirit crushed, one's imagination surpassed. One looks, one admires, and, seized with respect, one is silent. For where are the words to praise a work of art that may not have its equal anywhere on the globe?

After the death of Suryavarman II in about 1145, Angkor, and in particular its waterworks, is believed to have fallen into decay, with stagnant, untended canals becoming a breeding-ground for malaria. In 1177 and 1178 the Chams invaded and pillaged Angkor. In 1181, however, Jayavarman VII assumed kingship after a bloody war against the Chams. Possibly a usurper, he was a devout follower of Mahayana Buddhism, integrating its teachings with his idea of kingship, and identifying himself as a *bodhisattva*, an individual who has attained enlightenment but refuses to pass into Nirvana, choosing instead to contribute to the enlightenment of other mortals. Jayavarman VII's contribution to Angkor was the Bayon, a temple consisting of a series of towers crowned with immense human faces directed to all four cardinal points. Although much of the religious imagery is Hindu in inspiration, the bas-reliefs of the Bayon clearly celebrate the war against the Chams and illustrate scenes from daily life. The Bayon admits of more than one interpretation. On one level, the faces represent the Hindu god Brahma, who sees in all four directions. On another, it is Buddha Lokesvara, who sends his merciful gaze to all points of the compass. Finally, it is Jayavarman VII himself as bodhisattva, bestowing his benevolence on all his realm.

Jayavarman VII as a bodhisattva. This Khmer king, who reigned in the twelfth and thirteenth centuries, was a devout Buddhist, but also patronized Hinduism.

A bas-relief *(left)* from the thirteenth-century Bayon at Angkor *(opposite)* represents fighting between the Khmers and the Chams. Prominent are the royal war elephants, a typical feature of Southeast Asian conflict. *(Below)* The wise Ganesha, a son of the Hindu god Siva, with the head of an elephant and the body of a human, appears here in the style of the Bayon.

Jayavarman VII complemented this work with construction of hospitals and inns; an inscription describes his piety:

Filled with a deep sympathy for the good of the world, the king swore this oath: 'All the beings who are plunged in the ocean of existence, may I draw them out by virtue of this good work. And may the kings of Cambodia who come after me…attain with their wives, dignitaries and friends, the place of deliverance where there is no more illness.'

Jayavarman VII was the last king to build at Angkor; power relations shifted and following generations abandoned the site. In the late fourteenth century, Siamese invaders sacked the city; Cambodian kings returned for a brief period in the sixteenth century. French visitors in the nineteenth century 'rediscovered' it (although the Khmers had never forgotten Angkor),

Angkor returns to the jungle as a giant tree grows through the doorway to one of Jayavarman VII's temples. Once the Cambodian kings had abandoned Angkor, even the most magnificent temples fell prey to invading vegetation, water and other damage. Restoration and preservation are ongoing tasks.

and archaeologists undertook restoration of the huge complex. Unfortunately, the Indochina wars in the twentieth century again took a toll of the monuments and subsequent neglect brought more damage to these priceless remains.

Why was Angkor finally abandoned? The kings of Angkor had been able to build such great monuments because they controlled not only Khmer labour from the agricultural region around the Great Lake, but ample slaves who had been captured in wars with their neighbours. Possibly they also requisitioned non-Khmer forest peoples from within the realm. Construction thus depended on warfare, but wars were not always victorious. The Khmers now suffered attacks from the Siamese to the west, from the Chams and, later, the Vietnamese to the east. Furthermore, trade in Southeast Asia increased after the fourteenth century, but Angkor was in no position to participate in overseas commerce. The capital moved near to modern Phnom Penh, a better site for trade. Finally, and perhaps most decisively, Theravada Buddhism came to be the dominant religion of the Khmers. Its otherworldly orientation needed no elaborate kingly monuments. Nevertheless, Angkorean kingship was a model for later mainland kingdoms and Khmer pilgrims continued to worship at the site.

## EARLY JAVANESE KINGDOMS

The oldest known inscriptions from a Javanese kingdom are those of the fifth-century ruler of Taruma, Purnavarman, who resided not far from modern Jakarta. He left an inscription associating himself with Vishnu, carved in stone and adorned with his footprints and those of his elephant. Purnavarman's most important work, however, was to build a canal changing the course of the Cakung River, draining a coastal area for agriculture and settlement. Taruma soon disappeared from the scene, but Purnavarman's hydraulic achievement remains.

Chronologically the next centre of monument-building was the volcanic Dieng Plateau in central Java, where buildings date from the eighth century. Neighbouring south central Java, below the still-active volcano Mount Merapi, soon became the site of dozens of *candi* or shrines built to glorify deceased rulers. Hindu and Buddhist themes co-exist, temporally and spatially, yet there is no mixing of religious styles (as happened later). By the early tenth century, temple-building stopped in this area, and the centre of activity moved to eastern Java.

Like Angkor's rulers, those of Java identified in life with Hindu deities like Siva or Vishnu, and in death they were thought to be reunited with the deity in a statue of the god placed in the candi, which was both tomb and memorial. A candi, like Angkor's temples, represents Mount Meru, the centre of the cosmos. Externally, also like Angkor's edifices, the candis were lavishly decorated with bas-reliefs and carvings showing religious and mythical figures.

The temples of Dieng are attributed to a larger agriculture-based kingdom that appeared in Java some decades after Srivijaya established itself in Sumatra. An inscription of 732 praises a ruler named Sanjaya, who seems to have been responsible for early monument-building. A ruling family called Sailendra ('lord of the mountain') subsequently won hegemony in much of central Java and left Dieng behind. Patrons of Buddhism, the Sailendras appear to have subjected the Sanjayas, although this is not certain. They rebuilt existing Buddhist monuments and modified Hindu shrines to represent Buddhist concepts. Above all, they constructed Indonesia's most famous monument, Borobudur.

Major Hindu and Buddhist temples in central Java. Dozens of monuments were built in this area between the eighth and tenth centuries.

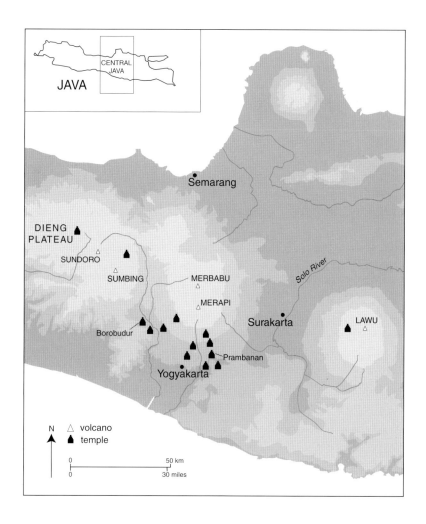

## BOROBUDUR

Not far from the present-day city of Yogyakarta in the plains of south central Java, this edifice was begun around AD 760, probably as a non-Buddhist shrine. Built around a hill, it was initially left unfinished. The Sailendras adapted this existing structure by widening its foundation and increasing the number of terraces. Stupas containing images of the Buddha, arranged in concentric circles, formed the uppermost terrace, while smaller Buddha images lined the galleries of the lower ones. Atop the structure was a large, empty stupa. Construction, once resumed, took about fifty years, until 830.

Tantrism, a variant of Buddhism that uses esoteric practices and meditative devices like mandalas to shorten the path to enlightenment, had spread to Indonesia soon after it appeared in the seventh century. Early Javanese Buddhism emphasized mandalas; the ground plan of Borobudur forms one, a geometric figure with Buddhas in concentric circles, concentrating power and eliminating evil influences.

Visiting Borobudur, the devout would not climb directly to the level of the stupas but rather traversed galleries on the rectangular terraces that are lined with bas-reliefs depicting Buddhist themes. The ascending sequence of reliefs takes the believer from earthly life to enlightenment, beyond which, in the stupas, is the Buddha himself. These didactic aspects, in addition to self-representation, were unquestionably important for the Sailendra rulers.

The lowest level of bas-reliefs portrays earthly misdeeds and the punishments that await them, a prelude to the appearance of the Buddha. This level was later covered, apparently for structural reasons, not out of prudishness. The visible terraces continue with scenes from the Jataka tales, which relate the lives of the Buddha before he was born as a prince. Then follow lives of other Buddhist models.

Such reliefs were common in India, but the idea of telling a story by placing the depictions in a line was a Javanese innovation. The visitor who follows the story also circumambulates the monument in a clockwise direction, in itself a pious exercise. These reliefs reflect much of daily life: handicrafts and trades, agriculture, clothing, the arts, plants and animals. Agricultural scenes show rice cultivation and transplantation of seedlings, practised in wet-rice areas today as it was in the ninth century in south central Java.

An engraving of Borobudur from a German children's book of 1821 shows that the great monument had already captured Europeans' fancy. The inset depicts – not quite correctly – one of the many stupas near the summit that contain (or formerly contained, for some have been removed or lost) a statue of the Buddha.

One of the uppermost levels of the Borobudur, with its many stupas containing half-concealed images of the Buddha. One of these is partially destroyed, allowing a clear view of the statue. Once brightly painted, the edifice still dominates the Javanese landscape.

In this bas-relief from a lower level of the Borobudur, two elephants come into view while in the treetops, monkeys are at play. The picture reflects the charming naturalism of the monument's extensive reliefs, especially those at the lower levels, which relate the stories of the Buddha's previous incarnations.

The finished structure, built around a natural hill, dominated the countryside. Once colourfully painted, Borobudur would have been strikingly visible from a considerable distance. The immense task of its construction must have tried the population of the area. Yet one expert has estimated that the task was perhaps not as mammoth as it first appears. Some two hundred labourers, working for half the year, could have built it within fifty years, although the number of artists and sculptors required remains unknown. Evidence of a good-sized village has been uncovered nearby, but there were no cities in the area.

Borobudur later lost its significance, becoming finally redundant with the Islamization of Java after the fourteenth century. Colonial officials discovered it in the nineteenth century, by which time it was in danger of collapse because rain water, seeping into the hill below, had washed away its support. Dutch archaeologists undertook a major restoration at the beginning of the twentieth century, but decay resumed until, during the 1970s, the Indonesian Archaeological Service, with the help of UNESCO, restored the edifice and secured Borobudur for subsequent generations.

## PRAMBANAN

Thirty temple sites have been discovered within a five kilometre (three mile) radius of Borobudur, most of them Hindu. In 825, a reaction against Buddhism seems to have set in, coinciding with the return of the Sanjayas. They did not destroy or change Buddhist structures (in fact they continued to build them into the late ninth century), but they added important Hindu temples. The largest of these is the Lara Jonggrang complex at the village of Prambanan.

At about this time, rule passed to Rakai Pikatan, a Hindu whose wife was Buddhist; he may have been a Sanjaya who married a Sailendra princess. Pikatan sponsored monuments to both faiths, including the Hindu Prambanan complex, finished in 856, not long after Borobudur was completed. Information from an Indian text suggests that the heirs of the Sailendras subsequently moved to Sumatra, becoming rulers of Srivijaya and leaving Java to Pikatan.

Lara Jonggrang, the 'slender maiden', who in Javanese tradition is a princess turned to stone by a rejected suitor, is in reality a beautiful statue of Durga, consort of the god Siva. To him the largest temple of the complex is dedicated. The central shrine of the complex, however, is a small stone shrine, perhaps for a local earth deity. Other large candi are for Vishnu and Brahma. Smaller candi were dedicated to the mounts of the three deities: Garuda (an eagle) for Vishnu, Nandin (a bull) for Siva, and Angsa (a goose) for Brahma. This upper level of the complex probably represents Mount Meru as the abode of the gods, as do Angkor Wat and other temples. At a lower level, additional edifices were erected by nobles of the kingdom. The non-symmetric arrangement of these smaller chapels reflects the geographic location of these nobles within the realm. Thus Prambanan is also a representation of the kingdom itself and, with that, a mandala, reflecting symmetry between the cosmos, the realm and the temple complex.

Siva, the central deity and one most often identified with rulers, is accompanied in his temple not only by his consort, Durga, but by his teacher Agastya and by the wise, elephant-faced Ganesha. This quartet of deities is often placed together in Javanese religion, but never so combined in other Hindu areas. Similarly, although

*(Below left)* The 'Slender Maiden', Lara Jonggrang, who gives her name to the ninth-century Prambanan temple complex, is in reality a beautiful statue of Durga, a consort of Siva. *(Below right)* Nandin (or Nandi), the bull, is the mount of the god Siva; this life-size statue found at Prambanan is the only one of a godly mount to survive relatively intact. His smooth appearance is said by some to reflect specifically Javanese aesthetic ideals.

The Brahma temple at Prambanan. The tallest, central temple of the complex is dedicated to Siva and represents Mount Meru, the centre of the universe in both Hindu and Buddhist cosmology; the entire site is also a representation of the central Javanese realm.

This covered bowl with a leaf design is part of the tenth-century golden treasure unearthed at Wonoboyo, near Prambanan, in 1990. The artifacts were buried by debris from a volcanic eruption.

Indonesian statuary follows the iconographic example of India, statues are more slender than the voluptuous Indian models.

In 1990 a chance find of gold and silver objects dating to about AD 900, buried by a volcanic eruption, shed new light on Javanese art. The location of the find, Wonoboyo, is only five kilometres (three miles) from the temple complex at Prambanan. Interestingly, Java has no gold deposits, so it must have tapped sources of precious metals in Sumatra or possibly Borneo. Some gold objects imitate nature: a golden water dipper is in the form of a palm-leaf dipper used by villagers. A lotus bowl of thin gold replicates Chinese porcelain. Most exciting perhaps is a vessel decorated with scenes from the *Ramayana*. It seems to have been intended for use in religious ceremonies, perhaps for Vishnu worship, since

Rama is an incarnation of Vishnu. Although much remains to be explained, visitors to the collection in the Jakarta Museum can confirm the skill and aesthetic capability of Javanese metalworkers as expressed in these objects so fortunately preserved.

In 919 building activity ceased in central Java for reasons not fully explained, although the location near the volcano Merapi suggests that an eruption could have led to flight. Other explanations (plague, war) are possible. Perhaps the population was simply exhausted by all the building activity and demanded a rest. By 928, Java's rulers had established their base in eastern Java.

## EASTERN JAVA

Whatever motivated the shift to the east, it meant the end of the great monuments, although Indian-influenced statuary and smaller temples continued to develop in the new locations. The shift to eastern Java also accompanied changes in long-distance trade. Under the Song Dynasty, China's demand for exotic foreign goods, especially for spices, greatly increased. Rulers in eastern Java were in a far better position than Srivijaya to control the spice trade, for the Spice Islands are in eastern Indonesia; they could also access the fertile rice-producing Brantas River valley. Between 990 and 1007, this area warred with Srivijaya, probably for control of trade.

One of the important rulers of the east, Airlangga (r. 1016–49), was the son of a Balinese ruler. Among his feats were the conquest of central Java and of Bali; he also tamed the Brantas River, making it possible to irrigate rice, and established a harbour not far from modern Surabaya. Able to control piracy, he guaranteed safety for international shipping, which gladly visited his new port. Airlangga divided his realm between two sons, establishing the kingdoms of Kediri and Singhasari.

In the late thirteenth century, this division ended when Singhasari overcame Kediri. The first ruler of the united kingdom was Kertanegara (r. 1268–92), who conquered Bali and established hegemony over Srivijaya, now based at Jambi-Melayu. Most Indonesians remember Kertanegara for the rebuff he delivered to a mission from the Mongol emperor Kubilai Khan to Java in 1289. Kertanegara captured and tattooed the Khan's legates, sending them back to China humiliated. When the Mongols responded by sending an enormous fleet to Java, Kertanegara was already dead. His successor was Raden Vijaya, who had established a new capital at Majapahit ('bitter gourd') in 1294. Raden Vijaya was able to convince

the Mongols that their enemy was his as well. Then he attacked them, catching them off guard and driving them away.

In eastern Java, religious styles mixed. The father of Kertanegara patronized Sivaism, Buddhism, Tantrism and other beliefs. After his death, his ashes were deposited in both a Siva and a Buddha temple, suggesting he identified with both. Sculpture began to deviate from classic models and temple building was decentralized, one reason why there are no great monuments in the area. Statuary became more 'Javanese', and many images of gods, especially Vishnu or Harihara (Siva-Vishnu), are thought to be portraits of individual deceased kings.

The carved balustrade of Candi Mendut, with bas-reliefs. Candi Mendut is one of many monuments built in central Java, not far from Borobudur and Prambanan, before AD 919. The devout still place flowers before its imposing statue of the Buddha, flanked by two bodhisattvas.

## MAJAPAHIT

The literary heritage of Majapahit includes the long poem *Negarakertagama* (properly called *Desawarnana*), written in 1365 by a Buddhist official, Mpu Prapanca. In addition to recording the king's splendour, as in the example of Hayam Wuruk's procession quoted above (p. 37), the poem lists the areas subject to Majapahit. Although it directly administered only eastern Java and Bali, Majapahit's territorial mandala extended from New Guinea and the Spice Islands to Sumatra and the Malayan Peninsula. In addition, Majapahit maintained relations with Vietnam, China and Thailand.

Hayam Wuruk came to power in 1350 at the age of sixteen, succeeding his mother, who ruled as queen for several years before abdicating on her son's behalf. The best-known ruler of Majapahit, he patronized Hinduism and Buddhism, as the *Negarakertagama* indicates. On his travels, he was accompanied by the author of the poem, Mpu Prapanca, and by Gajah Mada, his capable chief minister, an official who was largely responsible for the expansion of the dominions.

Majapahit was not only important because of the extent of its power. This was a time of beginning urbanization and flourishing trade. Taxes and fines were paid in cash. In about 1300, Chinese copper cash replaced the mostly gold and silver indigenous coins, probably because coins of small denominations were needed for monetized transactions. At Majapahit sites, a wealth of clay and terracotta objects – from images of people, animals and houses to toys for children – have been uncovered. Pottery remains, mostly found around the site of the court in modern Trowulan, offer a glimpse of everyday life; they even include banks for saving coins in the form of swaybacked Indonesian pigs.

The flourishing of the spice trade and renewed Chinese interest in the region, as well as the expansion of Islam, brought new rivals to the fore. By the fourteenth century, new trends were changing Java. Archaeological excavations at Trowulan have unearthed evidence of Muslim settlers, perhaps even members of court. Port cities along the north coast of Java, coming more strongly under Islamic influence, were divorcing themselves from Majapahit, while the Sultanate of Malacca competed for trade. In 1527, Majapahit fell to a coalition of new, Islamic harbour states from the north coast. Some of the royal family fled to Bali.

Trowulan was a centre of religious and civil administration, but also increasingly absorbed foreign settlers – Indians, Khmers, Siamese and Chinese. Majapahit's economy was both agriculture-based, taking advantage of east Java's fertile fields, and trade-based, the city acting as an entrepôt for the international spice trade and a major exporter of rice to nearby territories. Royal legitimacy, however, derived more from control of agriculture and from ensuring good harvests than from control of trade.

Geographically Southeast Asia's most extensive historical realm, Majapahit plays a role in national sentiment today. Indonesia's national motto, *Bhinekka Tunggal Ika* ('unity in diversity'), comes from a Majapahit text. In the twentieth century Indonesian nationalists saw Majapahit as a symbolic predecessor to the modern nation, pointing to its extent to legitimize their inclusion of the Spice Islands and West New Guinea in the Indonesian nation and arguing that

*(Opposite)* In this thirteenth-century sculpture from Singhasari in eastern Java, King Anusapatha is represented as Siva-Mahadewa (great god). The deity, in a meditative pose, carries the symbols of his might in two of his four arms: a fly-whisk and a circle of prayer beads.

The slit in the back of this fourteenth-century terracotta animal confirms its use as a piggy bank. Chinese copper coins (with their typical square holes) became the popular currency of Majapahit as both internal and external trade expanded and the use of money spread.

The kingdom of Majapahit in the mid-fourteenth century, with its core area and far-reaching subordinate territories.

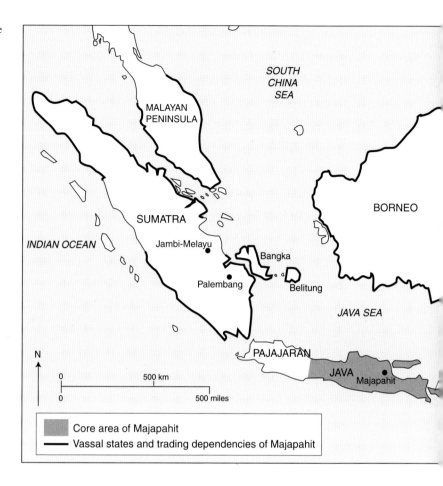

the nation derived somehow from this historical ancestor. The Republic of Indonesia memorialized Majapahit's great chief minister in the first university founded after independence, Gajah Mada University in Yogyakarta.

## PAGAN AND BURMA

The earliest known political units on the territory of present-day Burma, dating from the second century BC to the ninth century AD, were the settlements of the Pyus, often called 'proto-Burmans', along the upper Irrawaddy River, while the Mons or Talaing lived in the lower Irrawaddy valley and in parts of present-day Thailand. The Pyus seem to have practised Mahayana Buddhism, Hinduism and probably Theravada Buddhism, while the Mons are considered to have been the first Southeast Asians to adopt Theravada Buddhism.

By the eleventh century, Burmans controlled the rice bowls of upper Burma, and the fall of the Pyu to incursions from southern

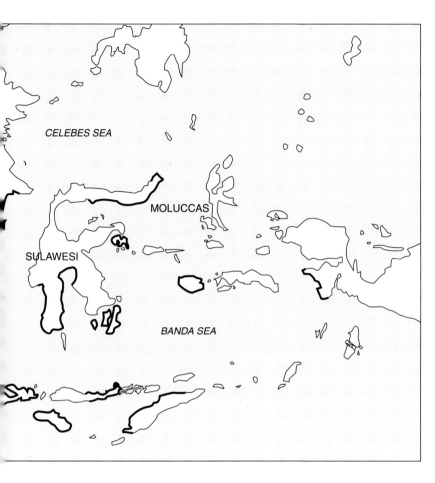

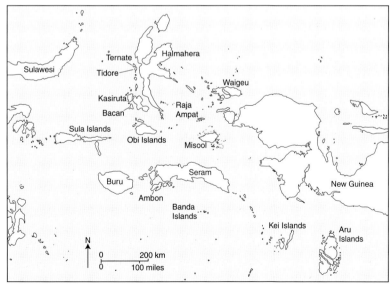

The Moluccas or Spice Islands.

In the eleventh century, Pagan
was the capital of Burma and a
centre of pious construction.
Thousands of temples and other
edifices were built. Towering over
them all is the white Ananda
temple, a masterpiece of Burmese
architecture.

China gave the Burmans the chance to establish power at their own
capital, Pagan, from which they soon expanded toward the coast.
The Pagan kingdom absorbed strong influences from both the Pyus
and the Mons, whose religion and writing system the Burmans
adopted.

Pagan's first king, Anoratha (r. 1044–77), is said to have converted
to Theravada Buddhism, but other beliefs persisted. His son
Kyanzittha (r. 1084–1113) completed the building of the Shwezigon
pagoda, a shrine for relics of the Buddha, including a tooth brought
from Sri Lanka (Ceylon). This edifice also houses images of thirty-
two nats, animist spirits that populate the Burmese countryside.
Kyanzittha's various inscriptions refer to him as an incarnation of
Vishnu, a chakravartin (universal monarch), a bodhisattva, and
*dharmaraja*, king of the (Buddhist) moral law. Ensuring legitimacy
apparently required resort to as many spiritual sources as possible.
His second great edifice, the Ananda temple, which the French
historian George Coedès calls the '*chef d'oeuvre* of Burmese
architecture', is possibly a funerary temple like those of Angkor or
Java, representing the king's passage to immortality.

During much of the twelfth century, anarchy reigned in Pagan.
Then in 1190 Anoratha's lineage regained control with the help of

Sri Lanka and brought about a reform of Buddhism on Sri Lankan models. Like Angkor, another inland agrarian polity that subdued coastal areas, Pagan left a splendid heritage of monumental architecture: there are thousands of smaller pagodas in addition to the grand royal ones. Narapatisithu (r. *c.* 1173–1211), the last important king, presided over a final transition to Burman cultural dominance. He also sought to deal with problems resulting from a Buddhist piety that transferred land to monasteries and so exempted it from royal control and taxation by reforming the *sangha* or monkhood and confiscating monastic estates.

Narapatisithu brought Pagan to new power, but the problem of land falling to the monasteries reappeared and his successors failed to assert their authority. This contradiction between Buddhist piety and royal power may have contributed to Pagan's eventual downfall in the thirteenth century, but internal divisions and events on the periphery like Tai and Mongol incursions were also to blame. A Tai people, the Shans, were beginning to enter Burma's lowlands from mountains to the east and north around this time. Mongol expeditions moved toward Pagan, ending with its capture and fall in 1287. The Shans eventually forced out the Mongols in the early fourteenth century, but Pagan was reduced to merely local significance, while

Buddhist statuary at the Shwezigon pagoda in Rangoon, photographed in *c.* 1885. According to legend the shrine was first constructed 2,500 years ago, when the Mons ruled southern Burma. It is believed to house eight hairs of the Buddha and relics of his predecessor-Buddhas, who lived thousands of years earlier. Shwezigon was an important religious site long before Rangoon was founded in the eighteenth century.

the Shans situated their capital at Ava. The next centuries saw division, conflict and disorder. A Burman polity finally reappeared at Toungoo on the Sittang River in the sixteenth century, where the Toungoo dynasty took power and assumed the task of reasserting Burman rule.

## A TAI CENTURY

The collapse of Pagan, and that of Angkor, brought Tai kingdoms to the fore. The Shan capital at Ava replaced the authority of Pagan in upper Burma. Even Srivijaya suffered from Tai expansion on the Malayan Peninsula, while these newly self-conscious peoples attacked Angkor and pushed back its boundaries. David Wyatt has called the period 1200–1351 a 'Tai century'. Hand-in-hand with Tai expansion and their formation of new states went the consolidation of Theravada Buddhism and the spread of monastic institutions among these former mountain peoples.

The most important expansion of a Tai people was that of the Siamese into the fertile rice-growing lowlands of present-day Thailand, areas then inhabited by Mons (about whose early kingdoms little is known) or ruled by Angkor, which controlled territories reaching to northern Thailand and much of Laos, where the population was not Khmer. The bas-reliefs of Angkor Wat portray Siamese troops, perhaps captives, who fought in the armies of Suryavarman II.

Although a northern Tai kingdom, Lan Na, existed in Chieng Mai from 1292, the kingdom of Sukhothai is considered the earliest predecessor of Siam-Thailand. A core of Tai elite grew up in the mid-thirteenth century southeast of Lan Na, in the Chaophraya valley, not far from Angkor and under the cultural influence of the Khmers and Mons. In the inscriptions of neighbouring states, as in Angkor, these people are known as Syam, or Siamese.

A slender bronze Buddha in the style of Sukhothai. Adoption of Theravada Buddhism opened new perspectives for the Tai, who in the thirteenth century were expanding their influence in mainland Southeast Asia.

Sukhothai's' third and most famous ruler, Ramkhamhaeng, 'Rama the Bold' (r. *c.* 1279–98) was able to take advantage of Angkor's weakness to make his kingdom a major power on the mainland. Ramkhamhaeng identified his new state closely with Theravada Buddhism; monarchy and sangha supported one another. He subdued, or made vassals of, rulers in Laos, much of modern Thailand, Pegu in modern Burma, and parts of the Malayan Peninsula. This expansion was not so much territorial conquest as the wholesale incorporation of other realms, which in turn brought the loyalty of their subordinates, and so on. The result was a mandala or galactic polity of centre and peripheries, cemented by pyramids of patrons and clients similar to those in many modern Southeast Asian societies.

Ramkhamhaeng's power was not only military; it was based on moral prestige as well, something his support of Buddhism confirmed in the eyes of his subordinates. His patronage and that of his successors gave rise to the Buddhist-influenced Sukhothai artistic tradition. His sculptors also still cast images of Vishnu and Siva, showing the continued influence of Hinduism at the court.

After Ramkhamhaeng's death, Sukhothai lost control of its territories as its vassals became independent. The mandala receded. Although now divided into many principalities, the Tai nonetheless remained important actors on the mainland scene.

## AYUDHYA

In 1351, U Thong, possibly the son of a Chinese merchant family that had married into the local elite, established Ayudhya as his capital and took the name of Ramathibodi. Its location on the Chaophraya River enabled Ayudhya to take advantage of the contemporary increase in international trade. Ramathibodi's links to the Chinese community would have reinforced this advantage. By the fifteenth century, Ayudhya was in close commercial contact, and sometimes competition, with Malacca, the Malay entrepôt on the Straits of Malacca.

In administration, Ayudhya adopted Khmer institutions, giving the realm a more structured authority than its predecessors. Successor kings were responsible for an increasing hierarchization of society, probably also evidence of Khmer influence, for traditional Tai societies had been more egalitarian. The backbone of Ayudhya's power was Tai military strength. By the early sixteenth century, Ayudhya, now virtually an empire, was the strongest power on the

A giant but ascetically thin reclining Buddha, his head resting on lotus flowers, illustrates Siamese Buddhist art from the Ayudhya period.

mainland. Its culture, incorporating Khmer, Mon and Tai elements, was now confidently Siamese.

Meanwhile, the new Burman state at Toungoo and Ava had gradually gained power, expanding at the expense of its Shan and Mon rivals. It would be the major challenger of Ayudhya for more than two centuries, repeatedly invading and being invaded.

### THE INDIAN LEGACY

Borrowings from Indian religion and culture are a key theme in much of the above discussion. Yet nowhere in Southeast Asia were Indian models adopted wholesale, not even in supposedly Hindu Bali. Indian influences, apparently so strong in writing, language, architecture and religious and political discourse, were in the end absorbed into primarily Southeast Asian cultures, contributing to but not replacing them.

Some authors believe that the early Indian religions were essentially a means to legitimize kings and kingship, and that their influence was limited to the upper classes. Yet even if Mahayana Buddhism and Hinduism were for the most part religions of the elite, and temple-building was mostly an exercise of royalty and royal power, important legacies remain.

While all members of the Hindu trinity – Brahma, Vishnu and Siva – are reflected in Southeast Asian remains, Siva was the most widely venerated. Siva worship was closely linked to royal authority. Monarchs in Champa adopted the Siva cult in the second half of the fourth century, according to inscriptions. An emissary from Funan to a Chinese court reported that Siva worship dominated there. And Khmer rulers venerated and identified with Siva, first as a linga (phallus), then as a statue.

Fasting, meditation and the concentration of spiritual power were pursued by Khmer chiefs with the aim of drawing on cosmic power to enhance personal and kingly qualities. The prestige of identification with Siva probably passed to the king's kin and enabled him to construct ever more monuments, statues or lingas. Asceticism entered the religious practice of lesser men, too, and influenced other religions, including Islam.

Basic to Hinduism, but of little influence in Southeast Asia, was the idea of caste. In Indian society, the Brahmans or priests, the Vaisya or warriors, and the Sudra or farmers constitute the three major castes, and there are hundreds of sub-castes related to descent and profession, as well as groups whose supposedly impure occupations (such as the handling of leather or the slaughtering of animals) put them beyond caste. The result of deeds in previous existences, caste was not to be overcome.

In Southeast Asia's more fluent societies, caste meant little. Nonetheless, Brahmans – or self-styled Brahmans, since there is a tradition that the Brahman should not travel abroad – rapidly took over spiritual functions in Southeast Asia. Taruma, the late fifth-century kingdom in western Java, used Brahmans to ritually secure its hydraulic project, the diversion of a river. They assisted in legal questions, importing Indian law codes to Cambodia by the eighth century, and as scribes. Some may have engaged in commerce. Brahmans married into royal families, crossing a caste barrier and becoming highly influential. Even the Theravada Buddhist courts made use of Brahman astrologers. They were valued for their esoteric knowledge as recently as 1948, when Brahmans determined the auspicious time and date for Burma's ceremony of independence.

Burmese astrologers at the ceremony of Burma's independence. A living relic of Southeast Asia's era of Hindu monarchies, these Brahmans determined the auspicious moment for the transfer of sovereignty to the new republic on 4 January 1948 (see p. 151).

Only in a few areas has Hinduism has persisted as a popular belief. Pockets remain in Java, but the best-known example of Hinduism is on the island of Bali. Local tradition relates that, when Majapahit fell to advancing Islamic sultanates in the early sixteenth century, some of the Majapahit nobility fled to Bali in order to retain their beliefs. Although Hinduism on Bali predates the spread of Islam on Java, it remains linked with this flight. Castes do exist on Bali, but their hold is far weaker than in India.

An important vehicle of Hindu ideas were the *Ramayana* and *Mahabharata*, epic folk tales which both still appear widely in popular folk drama, tales and art, just as they were illustrated in the reliefs of Angkor Wat. The *Mahabharata* was known in Cambodia in the second half of the fifth century. The *Ramayana* continues to be popular in the *Reamker*, a retelling in Khmer. In Java, *wayang* (shadow puppet) performances of themes taken from both epics (with a preference for the *Mahabharata*) are common in village and urban life. In addition, new tales have been composed, putting the characters in new situations or elaborating on the originals. Thailand's *Ramakien* situates the *Ramayana* in Southeast Asia, not India. Stories are retold in modern literature and even in comic strips.

Although the great rice-based kingdoms and the god-kings have passed, Southeast Asians have not ceased to build monuments, if for new purposes. One notable recent effort was the 'monumentalization' of Jakarta by Indonesian President Sukarno during the 1960s. Some statues and edifices are political, some have religious purposes. In all countries in the region, nationalists have been eager to replace colonial structures with monuments representing their new self-definition.

## CHAPTER THREE

# Multiplicity of Beliefs
*The Religions of Southeast Asia*

The world's major religions meet in Southeast Asia, and often mix. Although Hinduism, Buddhism, Islam and Christianity penetrated the region, these belief systems seldom appear in a theologically 'pure' form, as preceding chapters have shown. Instead, indigenous traditions and mutual influences characterize religious practices in Southeast Asian societies; like believers anywhere, most pay little attention to doctrinal stringency, their main concerns being material improvement and spiritual release.

This chapter begins with Hinduism and Mahayana Buddhism, the faiths that were at their most influential in the period already covered by this book. It then looks at popular forms of religion and their influence in Southeast Asia since the thirteenth century, a period that coincides with the Mongol invasions, the expansion of the Tai peoples, and the beginning of Islamization in the Malay-Indonesian world.

## HINDUISM

In Southeast Asia's early kingdoms, individual monarchs were glorified through their identification with Buddha and with Hindu deities. Hinduism is still the vibrant, living religion of India, and is characterized by a wealth of beliefs and practices. Its traditions go back to about 800 BC, or even earlier, and it emphasizes the unity of all living beings, the inevitability of rebirth and the worship of a diverse pantheon of deities. Some Hindus see all these gods as manifestations of the trinity of Brahma, Siva and Vishnu, or even of a single deity. Some are atheists. Devoid of dogma or required ritual, Hinduism's diversity expresses itself in a wealth of custom,

In this Balinese cremation ceremony, a woman places offerings before a papier-mâché bull housing the corpse of a Brahman. Like Hindus elsewhere, Balinese cremate their dead, although the deceased are usually buried temporarily while the family gathers funds for a more elaborate ceremonial cremation. Members of other castes are now also cremated in bovine effigies.

tradition and literature. This variety probably made it appealing to the spiritually eclectic early rulers of Southeast Asia; its role there is discussed in Chapter Two.

### BUDDHISM

Hinduism's teachings greatly influenced Buddhism. The Buddha was a historical figure, a prince who lived along the present border of India and Nepal in the fifth (some sources say sixth) century BC. The central teaching of Buddhism is that karma, retribution for good or evil deeds, determines humans' situation both in life and after death, when they will be inevitably reborn. Meditation and asceticism can help individuals to escape this cycle of rebirth and suffering by bringing them to enlightenment, a state called Nirvana, where no suffering and no human attachments exist. Rebirth affects lower and higher beings alike, including gods, and there is no creator-god or other being directing the universe. There are only the cycles of birth and rebirth and the long-term world cycles of renewal and destruction. Buddha himself attained enlightenment, but he is not a god – even if sometimes his followers appear to treat him as one.

The teachings of the Buddha spread rapidly throughout India, although they failed to displace Hinduism and earlier beliefs there. Unlike Hinduism, Buddhism was a missionizing religion, and it soon spread to other Asian countries. It was probably merchants and itinerant preachers who brought these beliefs to Southeast Asia, in the first centuries AD at the latest. Buddhism is known to have been established in the Indonesian Archipelago by the fifth century, since statues of that period have been found.

The earliest form of Buddhism to reach the Southeast Asian region was Mahayana, the 'greater vehicle', although the texts of Mahayana Buddhism are considered to be younger than those on which Theravada Buddhism is based. Mahayana teachings open the way to enlightenment not just to a few ascetics, as in Theravada, but to many individuals. As a result, although there are monasteries and monks, they are less important than in Theravada societies, since the path to enlightenment is not limited to monks. Adherents of the Mahayana tradition venerate bodhisattvas, individuals who have attained enlightenment but remain in contact with the world in order to help others gain enlightenment as well. Mahayana Buddhism was the inspiration for great religious architecture in Java and at Angkor. It is still important in East Asia, but in much of Southeast Asia has now vanished. After the decline of Angkor and Majapahit in particular, Hinduism and Mahayana Buddhism alike lost relevance for most Southeast Asian societies. Vietnam remains an exception, explained by its close relationship and cultural interchange with China, where Mahayana beliefs also remain popular. For similar reasons, Vietnamese courts also emphasized Confucianist orthodoxy, a trend that reached a peak in the nineteenth century.

Indian and Central Asian Buddhists found a welcome in Vietnam (then a Chinese province) in the second and third centuries AD, when commerce and religion mingled along the coasts of what is now northern Vietnam. Both holy men and merchants taught the new doctrine and the earliest temples date from this era. From there, Buddhism diffused into southern China. At the same time, Buddhists also visited Vietnam from the north, from China itself. Among them, in the sixth century, were adherents of the Thien (Zen) school. The resulting influence of this meditational school increased monastic and other exchanges with China. It may be that Vietnamese areas adjacent to China, where Buddhism was also strongly entrenched, felt more loyal to China. Other regions, further from China and where a more pluralistic, frontier atmosphere prevailed, were the source of uprisings against Chinese authority.

Some observers assert that early forms of Hinduism and Buddhism remained the exclusive concern of rulers and religious adepts like priests and monks. Certainly, early temples were abodes for the god-king, and offered only enough room for a priest to perform offerings, not for an assembly of the faithful. Yet the attention that the kings of Srivijaya gave to promoting Buddhism and the visibility and accessibility of the Borobudur to visitors must have propagated these beliefs among a broader population. The common people may have retained earlier beliefs, but Buddhism in particular was highly successful in absorbing previously venerated deities: spirits of land and water like the nats of Burma; historic individuals; or other deities of pre-Buddhist, 'animist' traditions who even today are believed to inhabit the trees and beaches, seas and watercourses, mountains and caves of the Southeast Asian world. When Vietnam divided during the seventeenth and eighteenth centuries the Nguyen rulers of the south chose to support Mahayana Buddhism as an integrative ideology for the ethnically plural society of their kingdom, which was also populated by Chams and other minorities.

Another variant of Buddhism was Tantrism or Vajrayana ('Diamond Vehicle'). The tantra were esoteric Buddhist texts, and they emphasized the possibility of gaining enlightenment through mandalas and through ecstatic religious practices. Tantrism absorbed ideas from Hinduism. It was practised in Srivijaya and its successor states and among rulers in Java; it influenced the construction of Borobudur.

THERAVADA BUDDHISM

Theravada ('teaching of the elders') Buddhism, less often called Hinayana ('lesser vehicle'), became the dominant religion of most of mainland Southeast Asia, replacing Hinduism and previous Mahayana beliefs. Its sacred language is not Sanskrit but Pali. Earliest texts date from about the first century BC, but definitive reinterpretations came in the fifth century AD. A Sinhalese king resurrected the classical doctrine in the eleventh century, with the help, it is said, of monks from Pagan. Southeast Asian Buddhists later placed great emphasis on exchanges with Sri Lanka when they wished to restore or maintain orthodoxy.

Theravada Buddhism was probably first brought to mainland Southeast Asia by the Mons, whose kingdom was centred on the southern coast of Burma, at Thaton and Pegu, but who also extended through much of present-day Thailand. It was a Mon monk who converted the Burmese ruler of Pagan, Anoratha, to Theravada Buddhism, and the king's subsequent invasion of Thaton enabled him to bring additional monks and scriptures, as well as the royal family of Thaton, to Pagan. In spite of its role in propagating Theravada Buddhism, which by the late twelfth century had been strictly defined, Pagan's religion remained a mixture of beliefs for some time, although contacts between Burma and Sri Lanka continued to promote orthodoxy. By the thirteenth century, Theravada Buddhism was spreading throughout mainland Southeast Asia. Perhaps the disruption of the classical kingdoms like Angkor opened the opportunity for conversion. Theravada Buddhism now became a truly popular religion, entering the villages, appealing to individuals of all walks of life. It could survive where kingdoms fell, and it has, even to the present.

Apart from Mons, Khmers and Burmans, Theravada Buddhism seems to have appealed particularly to the Tai peoples – Siamese, Shans, Lao and others – whose homelands were in south China (where they are related to the Zhuang of Guangxi Province) and in the mountainous areas of Vietnam. The Tai had not previously adhered to a major religion.

Strictly speaking, the goal of Theravada Buddhists is the transcendence of suffering and of repeated rebirth through the attainment of enlightenment and Nirvana, the state beyond suffering and rebirth. Only a select few who have lived as monks can achieve enlightenment, not the laity, and not women, who must be reborn. Observers of practical, contemporary Buddhism believe that most faithful see Nirvana and even earthly perfection as a remote and probably unattainable goal. They hope simply for the reduction of suffering through ritual, meritorious deeds, and the avoidance of evil, in order to better their present earthly condition. As practised in Southeast Asian societies, Theravada Buddhism has a strong individualistic strain. Unlike Mahayana, it has no bodhisattvas who help others to achieve enlightenment; one travels the path to Nirvana alone. Theravada Buddhism has absorbed varieties of spirit worship, magic, astrology, and other non-orthodox beliefs.

Although royal patronage certainly aided the spread of the new teaching, the key institution of Theravada Buddhism is the sangha or monkhood. In the past, and in some villages today, virtually all males entered the monkhood, at least temporarily, as young boys.

A nineteenth-century Burmese palm-leaf manuscript, showing the Buddha and the places he visited during his earthly life. In the past, many Southeast Asian texts were written on this highly perishable material.

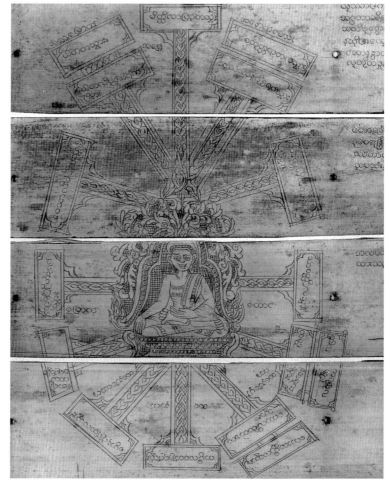

In an ordination ceremony in Thailand, a layman, dressed in white, receives the saffron robes he will wear as a monk.

Monasteries, located in the villages, were schools as well, and a large proportion of males in traditional Buddhist societies learned to read and write. Each day monks beg for their single meal, and the faithful can gain merit by filling their bowls. Often, adult men may retire temporarily to a monastery – a king might renounce his throne or, in modern times, a politician withdraw from public life and take the cloth. Young men may take orders to earn merit for their parents or benefactors. Buddhist festivals, ordinations and other feasts add colour and meaning to the calendar and to individual lives.

Rulers in Theravada Buddhist countries have often claimed the title of *dharmaraja*, king of the dharma or law, and with that the right to oversee the sangha and to legislate on religious matters. In Burma, kings exerted great efforts to submit the sangha to their discipline, and in the nineteenth and twentieth centuries Siamese kings adopted similar policies. The nineteenth-century Vietnamese Emperors Gia Long and Minh Mang also disciplined and regulated Buddhism, partly to ensure Confucianism's primacy.

Buddhist rulers had good reason to enforce religious discipline, for the sangha had a potential not only for amassing wealth and power at the expense of the court, but also for criticizing royal rule. One of the greatest king-reformers of Siam, Rama IV or Mongkut (r. 1851–68), was himself a member of the monkhood before his accession to the throne. A learned and cultivated man, he began, while still a monk, to reform the sangha in accordance with his understanding of the dharma or law and to open it to Western learning, a gradual process that continued into the twentieth century. His successors followed him in maintaining royal control of the sangha.

Using a boat for transportation, a Buddhist monk in Bangkok begs for food for himself and his fellow monks. Monks eat only one meal a day. By collecting their necessities from believers, they enable lay people to earn merit as well.

*(Right)* A Buddhist funeral procession in Vietnam.

*(Below)* A monk sets himself on fire at a main intersection of Saigon in 1963, in protest against the government of Ngo Dinh Diem (see p. 143).

*(Below right)* Former Thai military strongman Thanom Kittikachorn, exiled since the democratic transition of 1973, returned to take the cloth in 1976. Unimpressed by this display of piety, Bangkok students demonstrated against his return, provoking a brutal military response and the temporary end of the democratic experiment (see p. 162).

Even after the abolition of the absolute monarchy in Siam in 1932, the relation between Buddhism and power persisted. Ecclesiastical positions, examinations, religious schools and so on are under bureaucratic control, although the administrators may themselves be monks. Religious activities receive small subsidies, but state-financed education, usually better provisioned, competes with monastery schools. General Sarit, who held dictatorial power in the country from 1957 to 1963, propagated the slogan: King, Buddhism and Nation, appealing to religion, nationalism and the monarchy to legitimate his regime.

A more recent movement was the 'missionary monks' of the 1960s and beyond, whose mission was to promote government policy. Their task included both religious instruction and propagation of the goals of development and public health. In the face of regional dissatisfaction and unrest, they were also sent to preach to non-Buddhist hill tribes in order to ensure their loyalty to the nation. Lowland Buddhist peoples have tended, over centuries, to absorb hill peoples into their culture of sedentary agriculture and their religion of Theravada Buddhism. On the other hand, such proselytization can, as missions do, occasion hostility when it calls into question traditional cultures and insists that only the adoption of the majority culture and religion are appropriate to the nation.

Most Thais probably regard Buddhism as an integral part of their national identity, and confidently believe that conversion of non-Buddhist minorities is a necessary part of national integration. This opinion is shared by Burmese leaders like the former Prime Minister U Nu (in office 1948–58 and 1960–62). This devout leader repeatedly performed symbolic religious acts and eventually retired (temporarily) to a monastery. His strong emphasis on Buddhism as an integral part of Burmese nationhood contributed to the increased alienation of non-Buddhist minorities. The dictatorial military government led since 1962 by General Ne Win chose 'Burmese Way to Socialism' as a non-religious ideology for the regime. Nevertheless, this ideology reiterates Buddhist concepts of man and nature. When discipline among the monks became a problem, and some supported political protests, the military government tried to assert its authority over the sangha, first in 1965 and, more successfully, in 1980.

In Burma, politicization of the sangha is nothing new. By abolishing the Burmese monarchy, British colonial rule left no

*(Above)* Prime Minister U Nu's devotion to Buddhism and traditional beliefs sometimes mystified foreign observers, while his emphasis on the religion of the Burman majority alienated many of the country's non-Buddhist minorities.

*(Above right)* General Ne Win, military strongman and one of the Thirty Comrades (see p. 132) succeeded U Nu to the prime ministership in 1958. He later imposed strict rule over the sangha.

institution to ensure that a wearer of the yellow robe was a true man of religion. Monks were often badly trained and disciplined, while some used the freedom of the cloth to attack colonialism or for less worthy purposes – to hide from the law, for example. The military regime's attempts to assert its authority over the sangha were made not only for reasons of religious discipline, but to ensure that the sangha did not harbour anti-government elements.

Though many factors have changed the position of Buddhism in society, it continues to be a part of the life of most Thai, Burmese and – despite cultural upheaval, war and ideological struggles – Khmers and Laotians. In Laos, Communist rulers after 1975 attempted to change attitudes to religion, in particular calling on monks to work, not beg. This caused many to return to lay life, but Buddhism remains popular. Cambodia's terrible period of social revolution under the Khmer Rouge between 1975 and 1978 saw the destruction of temples and monasteries and the dispersal or murder of many monks. Buddhist practice is only slowly recovering from this trauma.

Buddhism was traditionally a rural institution, based in village monasteries and drawing its recruits from village youth. Urbanites do become monks, but in general only temporarily. Nonetheless,

Buddhism remains influential in Southeast Asian cities, as novel urban lay movements have sprung up to bring new impulses to Buddhist practice. This 'new middle-class' Buddhism, found in Thailand, may spread to other lands. In addition, monks in recent years have increasingly joined protest movements, adding a political quality to their position.

## CONFUCIANISM

Confucius lived in northeast China, probably in the sixth century BC. He left a body of ethical teachings to his disciples that would enable them to live in accordance with the way of Heaven, which is not, it seems, a god so much as an impersonal force. His teachings were the source for an extensive body of classical texts that in turn became the basis of the Chinese educational system. Although Confucianism is not usually considered to be a religion, there are Confucian temples in China and Vietnam. In Indonesia, a Confucian movement among the Chinese minority sought in the twentieth century to have this tradition recognized as a religion with worship of Heaven as a central ritual.

Confucianism, as a kind of secular religion, is rightly placed in a discussion of the Vietnamese monarchy over time, for, apart from

Gateway to the Van Miew (Temple of Literature), a Confucianist edifice in Hanoi. Southeast Asian Confucianism, practised by Chinese minorities and more widely in Vietnam, blurs the boundary between ethical system and popular religion.

among Chinese minorities throughout the region, it was only in Vietnam that Confucianism exercised influence. Even so, most Vietnamese (and most Chinese) held to a mixture of Mahayana Buddhist, Taoist and local animist beliefs as well as honouring Confucian ethics. Vietnamese kings in fact recognized the 'three beliefs', Confucianism, Taoism and Buddhism. Confucianism, with its emphasis on hierarchy and rationalism, was more a state philosophy than a popular religion. The system of education that inculcated Confucian orthodoxy was oriented to central examinations for entry to the bureaucracy. Introduced into Vietnam in the eleventh century, the examinations fell into disuse until they were regularized under the Le dynasty in the late fifteenth century. Under the nineteenth-century Nguyen, Vietnam's last independent rulers, Confucianism achieved its greatest influence, perhaps because the dynasty needed a firm basis to meet internal and external challenges.

Confucianism also regulates family life: the wife is to obey the husband, the son the father, the younger brother the older. Yet Vietnam always retained something of Southeast Asia, its women enjoying much greater freedom than their sisters to the north. Unlike in China, widows and even deserted wives were free to remarry. One fifteenth-century Chinese emperor, informed of such shocking behaviour, determined to uplift the morals of Vietnamese women and combat their un-Confucian mores by printing and distributing ten thousand copies of the *Biographies of Exemplary Women*, a bible of Confucian uprightness.

## TAOISM

Taoism (sometimes spelled Daoism) is, literally, the doctrine of the way (*dao*). Its probably mythical founder, Laozi, is supposed to have lived in the sixth century BC. While Confucius was concerned with family and state, Taoist philosophy rejects order and hierarchy for change and indeterminacy, defying definition. It contains elements of natural religion, finding special significance in bizarre forms of trees or rocks, for example, or in searching for the elixir of immortality.

Above all, Taoism is the popular religion of China. Chinese temples and houses are built according to Taoist principles, its religious specialists may be Taoist masters and most of the gods, including deified historical persons, are of Taoist origin. Chinese medicine and geomancy derive in large part from Taoist ideas of man and nature. In both China and Vietnam, Mahayana Buddhism and Taoism so influenced each other that it is difficult to distinguish them in practice. Outside of culturally sinicized areas, however, Taoism is unimportant.

Taoism entered Vietnam from China. Its quest for immortality through elixirs and other potent mixtures particularly appealed to native Vietnamese ideas about life. Understandably, Confucian rulers and bureaucrats often regarded Taoism as unorthodox and even politically subversive.

## ISLAM

Muslim traders from the west visited Southeast Asia some time after the founding of Islam in the seventh century AD and early Islamic centres soon existed in southern China. In the Archipelago, it was only in the thirteenth century that the first local Islamic kingdoms appeared, although an early Muslim tombstone found in eastern Java dates from the eleventh century. The first Islamic kingdom was Pasai, in northern Sumatra.

Many traditions influenced Islam in Southeast Asia, including those of the Arab world, Persia, India and probably China. Most believers adhere to Sunni Islam of the Syafi'i school, one of four legal traditions in Sunni Islam, but local beliefs have also absorbed Shiite elements and, above all, the mystical traditions of the Sufis. Like its predecessor religions, Islam assimilated many local influences as it spread.

Although Islam travelled different routes, sometimes converting rulers and entire populations in a single thrust, it was initially closely linked to the expansion of trade. In east Java by the fourteenth century, Muslims were among the elite at the capital of Majapahit. In addition, north Java's port cities converted and, as sultanates, competed with Majapahit for trade. New men, especially merchants and traders, many of them foreigners, formed the elites of these sultanates.

Islam's strongest expansion was during the sixteenth century, when it reached inland villagers of major islands of the Indonesian Archipelago. Conversions apparently moved in a northwest to southeast direction, and Aceh, in north Sumatra, was one of the earliest sites. Still one of the most strongly Islamic areas of the Archipelago, Aceh likes to call itself the 'veranda' of Mecca. Under

Sultan Iskandar Muda (r. 1607–36), Aceh reached the peak of its power, controlling a lucrative trade in pepper. From the north, Islam spread to other parts of Sumatra, including the neighbouring Minangkabau area in western Sumatra, then to hill peoples. It is still expanding today.

In Java, Islam took another path. Tradition ascribes the conversion of Java to the efforts of the Wali Sanga, nine saints or apostles, most of whom lived in the sixteenth century. According to legend (and sometimes history), some were Arabs, some Chinese, others Indians or Javanese. Their tombs are, even today, places of pilgrimage for believers. Veneration of tombs is not condoned in orthodox Sunni Islam; this shows the influence of other Islamic traditions or pre-Islamic practices.

Not surprisingly, early mosque construction continued the forms used in pre-Islamic architecture, down to tiered roofs and split gates known from Javanese and Balinese temples that represented the Hindu–Buddhist Mount Meru. The introduction of minarets and Near Eastern architectural styles is a relatively recent trend; in the

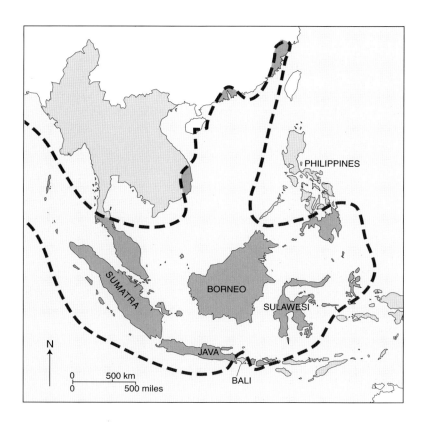

The extent of Islam in Southeast Asia and southern China.

twentieth century, many Muslims have striven to imitate closely 'authentic' Islamic forms.

Another important base of Islamization was the Sultanate of Malacca, which probably converted to Islam soon after it was founded in 1402. Its second ruler already bore an Islamic name. Until it was taken by the Portuguese in 1511, this sultanate controlled much of the trade passing the Straits of Malacca. In addition, Malacca was a centre of Malay culture and a model for subsequent Malay Muslim sultanates in the Peninsula, in Sumatra, and elsewhere. Islam finally reached what is now southern Thailand and the southern Philippines, where it was halted by Spanish expansion. Champa, too, was at least partly Islamized.

Islam changed the culture of maritime Southeast Asia in many ways. It brought a new system of writing; the Malay language was now written in Arabic script, called Jawi. Malay itself became the language of religious works, and, next to Arabic and Persian, a major vehicle of Islamic discourse. Poems, stories, treatises and commentaries appeared, and still appear, for believers. Art forms gradually adapted to Islamic examples, and representations of humans and animals were suppressed or greatly stylized. The dead were now

The mosque of Bandar Seri Begawan, Brunei, completed in 1992. While the earliest mosques in maritime Southeast Asia followed the architectural styles of Hindu temples or borrowed from styles in India, in recent years domes and minarets have come to predominate as Near Eastern influence grows.

Islamic aesthetics reshaped artistic tastes in strongly religious areas. The bird design on this Sumatran batik cloth is formed with squiggles resembling Arabic calligraphy. Earlier patterns were more realistic.

wrapped in a shroud and buried facing Mecca. Mosques were oriented to Mecca, which replaced royal cities as a new exemplary centre far outside Southeast Asia.

New institutions left their mark on local societies. The first was the traditional Islamic, usually rural, school, the *pesantren* or *madrasah*, where students lived with a master, studying the Koran and Islamic law. Their training emphasized self-reliance, and included practical skills such as growing crops or trading. Although Hinduism has similar institutions (called in Indonesian *asrama*), these traditional schools left a strong imprint. They are documented only from the eighteenth century but probably existed earlier. Students often travelled from one school to another, following a network of learned men. The masters – *ulama* (in Java also called *kiai*) – formed a special and greatly respected group; leading families often intermarried. Pesantren might also enjoy endowments of land or other resources that made them economically independent. Ulama, offering an alternative view of politics and ethics, might become critics of sultans and other rulers. Not surprisingly, pesantren have at times become alternative centres of legitimacy and religious teachers have often led rebellions against civil authority.

Despite the long and arduous journey, Southeast Asians have been frequent participants in the *haj*, the pilgrimage to Mecca. One of the first to visit the holy places was the sixteenth-century writer Hamzah Fansuri of Aceh. Later pilgrims would remain for several years near Mecca, and a colony of 'Jawi' (Indonesians) grew up there with its own teachers and specialists. In the early twentieth century, students also went to Cairo, where the Al-Azhar University offered insight into new trends in Islamic thinking. As a result, events in the Near East drew closer to Southeast Asia.

Another institution, sometimes linked with the Islamic schools, was that of the mystical Sufi brotherhoods. Students at religious schools might be inducted into these brotherhoods, or pilgrims to Mecca might become members during their stay in the holy places.

In no way is Southeast Asian Islam monolithic. Controversies divided the faithful in the past, and still do. Legal interpretations admit of differences; in the early decades of the twentieth century, a split between the traditionalists and those who wanted to reform Islamic practice, the so-called *kaum tua* (the old ones) and *kaum muda* (the young), affected many religious centres. In Java, a number of organizations crystallized out of this debate. One is the more traditional Nahdlatul Ulama (Association of Islamic Scholars), which adheres closely to a single Syafi'i school of legal interpretation but is nonetheless the more open to culturally Javanese accretions. Another is the Muhammadiyah, a modernist organization that has attempted to purify Islamic practice of traditional but non-Islamic elements. Muhammadiyah was among the pioneers of modern Islamic education. Both groups participate actively in contemporary Indonesian discussions about politics, society and the economy and their adherents have formed separate Islamic political parties.

Since the 1980s, a so-called Islamic revival has gathered force in Southeast Asia. *Dakwah* movements, a term that means something like preaching, or evangelization, have proliferated among the faithful. Islam takes an increasingly prominent position in public life, underlined by the relatively new but widespread use of headscarves among Muslim women, especially young women. Modest prosperity

Headscarves and computers: Malaysian university students illustrate different trends influencing modern young Malays. There is in fact no tradition of such scarves; to their wearers they represent Islamic modernity.

has brought more investment in religious activities of all kinds, including the haj, strict observance of fasting, and a proliferation of Islamic popular literature.

This revitalization of Islam is attributable to a range of factors: the role of religious instruction in national schools, which reach more and more of the region's children; government support for mosque-building and religious precepts; Near Eastern influences; and political uses of Islam. In Malaysia, the ruling UMNO party (United Malays' National Organization) has moved toward Islam in order to claim some of the territory of its competitor, the strongly Islamic PAS (Partai Islam SeMalaysia or Pan-Malaysian Islamic Party).

Indonesia officially recognizes five religions: Islam, Hinduism, Buddhism, Catholicism and Protestantism (these two are considered to be separate) and permits their open organization. However, Islam, as the religion of about eighty-five per cent of the population, obviously has the strongest claim to a say in public affairs. Politicians court the Islamic vote, although opposition to an Islamic state that would enforce religious precepts remains strong, not least because influential military officers recall the battles against separatist Islamic movements in the past. In recent years, some violent anti-Christian outbreaks, and fighting between Muslims and Christians, have marred Indonesia's reputation for religious tolerance.

## CHRISTIANITY

Like other major religions, Christianity entered Southeast Asia from overseas; but unlike them, it was brought by conquerors and colonizers. Christianity today is strongest in the Philippines, where the population is about eighty-five per cent Catholic, with a further ten per cent belonging to other Christian churches, including at least two native Philippine churches. Christians are found in significant numbers in eastern Indonesia; among the Toba and other Batak peoples of northeastern Sumatra; and in parts of Java, where significant Christian populations exist in most urban areas. In mainland Southeast Asia, Christian missionaries, meeting little success among the lowland Buddhist peoples, turned their attention to minority groups, mostly hill tribes. There is also a significant Catholic minority in Vietnam, estimated at six million.

The Christianization of the Philippines was the result of a consistent policy under three centuries of Spanish occupation. The Spanish left the administration and education of the countryside in the hands of the Catholic clergy and pursued policies strongly favourable to the Church. Nevertheless, the numbers of clergy – one

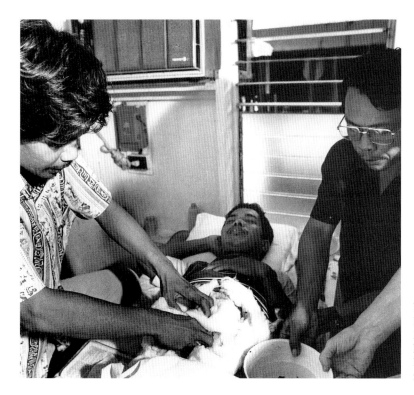

Unorthodox Christianity in the Philippines takes many forms. Here, a faith healer performs a knifeless 'operation' for which he and his followers claim miraculous cures.

In a rural mission school in North Borneo (now Sabah, part of Malaysia) a Catholic sister looks after children of both Western and Asian origin. Mission schools have traditionally been highly regarded in urban areas by Chinese and Indian minorities, and often by local people as well, attracting many pupils who were not members of Christian churches.

estimate is that no more than four hundred were active at any one time during the sixteenth and seventeenth centuries – were insufficient to achieve thorough cultural assimilation. Despite the widespread conversion of Filipinos, native religious beliefs have persisted alongside the new religion and coloured its practice. Philippine Catholics maintain many non-orthodox traditions, as do adherents of Islam and Buddhism in the rest of Southeast Asia. After the Spanish period, Philippine churches were founded to offer a kind of native Catholicism.

In all of Southeast Asia, missionary schools are popular in urban areas and still enjoy a good reputation. The spread of Christianity through education particularly reached minorities like the Chinese and Indians. Because of their relatively high levels of education, Christians have been influential beyond their numbers in countries like Indonesia. Some nationalistic governments, recalling the close relationship between colonialism and Christianity, have restricted the admission of foreign clergy and of funds from abroad. Christian churches in Southeast Asia today are for the most part local churches, with local clergy.

Cataclysm is about to come.
Sun and moon will change places in the sky, smoke will envelop the earth.
No house, no tree, no blade of grass will be left.
And then, there will be peace and perfect tranquillity.
    Prophecy of Huynh Phu So, leader of the Hoa Hao sect in Vietnam

All Southeast Asian belief systems lend themselves to the expectation that the world as it exists is about to end in disaster. Christians have the Second Coming of Christ, Muslims their Mahdi or future prophet. In Java, the tradition of a *ratu adil*, a just prince who would free his people, reinforced the idea of the Mahdi. Buddhist teaching also speaks of the destruction of the present era, coinciding with the rise of a new Buddha, Maitreya, who will usher in a new era.

In times of natural, political or economic crisis, holy men have repeatedly arisen, using religious symbols and traditions to promise ultimate release from current suffering, sometimes claiming to be the saviour themselves. In the approaching cataclysm, only the holy man's close adherents would be saved; their amulets, rituals or secret signs, which the purported redeemer gives them as protection and identification, would ward off evil.

Religion, especially peasant religion, also offered a vocabulary and a counterethic, even a utopia, against which to judge the state. The stresses of the nineteenth and early twentieth centuries, with new taxes and demands on labour from central authorities, or disruptions from warfare, famine, plague and dispossession, fed such movements among peasants. Millenarian beliefs flourished especially in border areas between ethnic groups or where groups mixed, and in places where heterodox or rebellious sects had deep roots. The exaggerated expectations of such movements, their lack of organization, and their dependence on personal attachment to a prophet-leader made most of them short-lived. Rarely did they upset the state more than locally or temporarily.

Millenarian ideas have survived in new forms. Not only Burman and Siamese kings but leaders of modern anticolonial movements often consciously referred to these traditions. A nationalist leader like Sukarno of Indonesia knew well how to assure his followers with promises of a golden age; these expectations accompanied the Indonesian nationalist movement and the fight for independence. With the abolition of the Burmese monarchy and consequent loss of central control over the sangha, individual monks, healers and holy men became leaders of millenarian and anticolonial

The all-seeing eye of the Cao Dai god recalls some Christian iconography. This symbol, however, is surrounded by Asian lotus blossoms.

movements, disrupting the authority of the British colonial regime.

Although Vietnamese culture seems to have been traditionally more secular, there, too, other-worldly movements found adherents. Not surprisingly, given the multicultural character of the south, they flourished there, while in the north, disaffected mandarins led more secular, political rebellions. Two noteworthy movements arose during the twentieth century from unorthodox political–religious traditions in southern Vietnam, where Vietnamese and Cambodian elements mingle and the pioneer character of the region created hardship and disaffection. The first, Cao Daiism, propagated syncretist religious ideas with an essentially Taoist base. It attempted to arrive at a synthesis of Asian and Western traditions, often appealing to an educated middle-class with some knowledge of French. Among its 'saints' are Buddha, Laozi and Confucius, as well as Jesus Christ, Victor Hugo and Joan of Arc, all under a Supreme Being pictured as an all-seeing eye.

The Buddhist sect of Hoa Hao was the successor to Buu Son Ky Huong ('Strange Fragrance from the Precious Mountain', a phrase signifying the people of southern Vietnam). This was a divergent Buddhist tradition long present in southern Vietnam. Hoa Hao was founded in 1939 by Huynh Phu So, who attracted many followers by both healing and preaching.

Both sects formed military units with Japanese help during World War II and began to control their own territory. Ngo Dinh Diem suppressed them forcibly in 1955, soon after he took office, but the sects have survived to the present. The Cao Dai temple in the province of Tay Ninh is an eclectic wonder and still a monastic centre, while the Hoa Hao continues to spread the teachings of its deceased Patriarch Huynh, although the government now strictly circumscribes the political and social influence of both sects.

## CHAPTER FOUR

# Southeast Asia as a Crossroads
## *Relations with China and European Advances*

Previous chapters have described early influences from India, China and the Near East on Southeast Asia. This region may be the part of the globe most affected by foreign influences. Although sometimes called an 'Asian Mediterranean', it is geographically even more open to the outside world. This is especially apparent in the early modern period, which bridged the time between the downfall of the 'classical' kingdoms and the consolidation of Western colonialism.

### CHINESE INFLUENCE

China's interest in Southeast Asia waxed and waned over the centuries. Its trade continued to be a motor of Southeast Asian economies, more important than trade with India or the West even as late as the early nineteenth century. From the time of the Song Dynasty (960–1278), Chinese ships or junks – which combined traits of Chinese river vessels with innovations from Malay sea-going ships – competed with Southeast Asian vessels as long-distance carriers. After the seventeenth century, Chinese junks replaced much native shipping.

A seventeenth-century depiction of a Chinese junk. Chinese vessels began to replace those of the Malays in long-distance trade with China after the tenth century. They eventually became dominant, and remained so well into the nineteenth century.

The Mongols (who ruled China from 1278 to 1368) attempted conquest; other dynasties were satisfied with trade. For Chinese officialdom, trade was part of the so-called tribute system that governed foreign relations. The Ming (1368–1644), however, were also interested in the security of long-distance Asian trade. Under the Ming Dynasty a flurry of important visits of fleets led by admiral Zheng He, a court eunuch and a Muslim, reawakened trade and interest in the south. Often known as Sam Po, Zheng is widely venerated within Southeast Asia, especially among the Chinese minorities, who have dedicated temples to him, usually near the sea coasts. The most important of these is in Semarang in central Java.

China's renewed attention probably helped make Malacca the dominant entrepôt in the region in the fifteenth century. Increased commerce also led many Chinese, not least members of Zheng He's fleet, to settle permanently in Southeast Asia, although in theory Chinese were not allowed to go abroad for private reasons, much less to remain there. The settlers married local women and established families; Chinese communities gradually formed at major trading ports and Chinese traders, craftsmen and market gardeners came to dominate much of the commerce at the major cities of the area. This process affected native ports and, later, European harbour settlements like Batavia and Manila.

Three Chinese pepper merchants at the market of Banten, west Java, in the late sixteenth century. On the left, the trader weighs a sack of pepper with his Chinese scales.

Where Chinese successfully settled in independent Southeast Asian kingdoms and sultanates, they often intermarried with the local elite, as was the case in Siam and Vietnam. Not even Islam was a barrier to this practice; Chinese or their progeny converted easily, perhaps because they knew Islam from their homeland. In sparsely populated areas of the region, Chinese settlers found a niche as producers of raw materials for the Chinese market, importing Chinese labourers to plant and work gambier (a vegetable dye used in tanning and dyeing), to mine gold and tin, or to grow pepper.

The Chinese stayed on, for the most part, when Western colonialism took over. By the time that colonial territories were consolidated, however, Southeast Asia's economic relations had changed decisively. China had been supplanted as the major trading power by Europe and North America.

## CHINA'S SPECIAL RELATIONSHIP WITH VIETNAM

The most important site of Chinese influence – economic, political and cultural – was Vietnam. Unlike other states in the region, and in large part because of its proximity to China, Vietnam has left a written record of its early history, even if these histories stress Confucian orthodoxy and are silent about other aspects of Vietnamese life.

Bronze-working at Dongson (see pp. 19–20) nearly coincides with the early kingdoms of Van Lang (c. 800–258 BC) and Au Lac (257–208 BC) in northern Vietnam. Under these kingdoms there was increasing social differentiation and agricultural intensification, perhaps even with irrigation and double-cropping of rice, something that would later become widespread in the more densely populated areas of Southeast Asia. Au Lac was conquered by a Chinese warlord who gave the name Nan Yue (Southern Yue or, in Vietnamese, Nam Viet) to his territories, a precursor of its current appellation, 'Vietnam'. Nam Viet included only the north of modern Vietnam, and with it, the Chinese provinces of Guangdong and Guangxi. In 111 BC, the Chinese emperor Wu of the Han Dynasty invaded Nam Viet and ended its semi-independence. Three Vietnamese provinces formed, Giao Chi (in Chinese, Jiaoji), Cuu Chan (Zhouzhau) and Nhat Nam (Rennan). To the south was what the Chinese called Linyi, probably one or more Cham kingdoms. In AD 40, two women, the Trung sisters, led a rebellion against Chinese rule. When they had finally suppressed the uprising, the Chinese absorbed the southern dominion as a province of China. Later, they would call Vietnam

'Annam', the pacified south. By that time, the capital was situated at Thang-long, close to modern Hanoi.

In the eleventh century, Vietnamese territory – still only the northern part of today's Vietnam – achieved its independence, taking the name Dai Viet (Greater Viet). Leaders of the struggle were a new nobility, aided by the Buddhist monkhood. Successive dynasties attempted to consolidate political and administrative order. Borrowings from Chinese culture, including organizational concepts, helped them establish independence from China. About half the vocabulary of modern Vietnamese is of Chinese origin, although the language is not Sinitic. Interaction with China, with neighbouring kingdoms, and probably with mountain peoples as well gave the Vietnamese a strong sense of their own distinct identity. These earliest centuries of independence were critical for Vietnamese self-definition.

The first independent dynasty was the Ly (1009–1225), whose rulers established not only a military but an administrative and cultural base for the state, relying at first on an alliance between military figures and the Buddhist monkhood. Vigorous leaders revised the legal codes and the tax systems and maintained trade relations with peoples in the interior. Ly emperors built temples and patronized Mahayana Buddhism, though they honoured the traditional spirits as well. Ly Nhat Ton (r. 1054–72) adopted court titles from China, and the Chinese noted that he called himself 'emperor', an offence in their eyes. Ly Nhat Ton attacked the Sino-Viet border in 1059, forcing the withdrawal of some expansionist Chinese officials in the area.

Like his grandfather, Ly Nhat Ton also waged war against Champa. This power to the south was an 'Indianized' kingdom (or maybe kingdoms – see p. 25). Champa too left its mark on Vietnamese culture, for the Vietnamese also defined themselves in relation to these southern neighbours – in opposition, or sometimes in imitation. And although Dai Viet is usually considered to have been a land-based, agrarian kingdom, trade also brought influences from far away.

This painted wooden statue, dressed in a silk garment, dates to eleventh- or twelfth-century Vietnam. The gentleman is believed to be a king of the Ly dynasty, the first dynasty of independent Vietnam.

The Song Dynasty emperors were unhappy with their independent-minded neighbour. After a number of border skirmishes in which the Vietnamese forced the Chinese to a standstill, the two parties finally agreed to delineate their border. By implication this meant that the Chinese emperor recognized Dai Viet as more than merely a vassal. And because border delineation was distinctly non-Southeast Asian, it forced Dai Viet for its part to acknowledge its special relationship with the empire to the north.

During this time, civil service examinations on the Chinese model were introduced, although the system soon fell into disuse. Among the achievements of the Ly was their affirmation of Buddhism. They also instituted 'a Vietnamized version of Chinese political theory' that made of the king a 'southern emperor', while China was subject to a 'northern emperor' whose power stopped at the Vietnamese border. Nevertheless, Dai Viet continued to send tribute to China. Ly kings continued to reign until 1225, but during the twelfth century the throne was repeatedly occupied by weak rulers, often mere children. By the thirteenth century, civil war prevailed.

The succeeding Tran dynasty (1225–1369) built up a fleet that, together with a strong army, enabled them to repel Mongol threats. By choosing queens only from their own family and by the ruler naming his heir on assumption of the throne (the reigning monarch was 'senior king'), the Tran avoided many pitfalls of Southeast Asian royal successions. In the 1230s, they re-introduced the Chinese examination system. This had the effect of creating a class of literati-officials whose culture was determined by their Confucian education; they were the forebears of Vietnam's mandarin elite. Challenged by the Mongols and threatened by invasions, the Tran successfully asserted that they were emperors too, not subject to the Chinese emperors.

When a Tran emperor took a concubine from another family, her kinsmen exploited the unrest of the late fourteenth century to seize the throne. A Cham king took advantage of the ensuing disorder to attack the kingdom and sack the capital, Thang-long. Quick in turn to seize the opportunity given by internal and external unrest, in 1406 the Ming rulers of China invaded. Their resources were not equal to the task of holding onto their prey, however, and in 1428 the last Chinese withdrew before the attacks of the forces of Le Loi, who became the founder of another dynasty.

The most prominent Le emperor was Le Thanh Ton (r. 1460–1497). His achievements included establishing a model bureaucracy, presiding over a time of great cultural flourishing in literature, history and law, and making significant territorial conquests in Laos and Champa. A few years after his death, however, civil war was rekindled.

Dai Viet's control of wet-rice agriculture and management of the periodic flooding of the Red River through a system of dikes enabled the land to support a dense population in the lowlands. Its manpower was an asset in the rivalry with Champa, and eventually led to the latter's disappearance, or rather absorption. In the seventeenth century, the Trinh achieved dominance in the north and were again able to enforce Confucianist ideals. The villages of the north were tightly organized and disciplined, a necessity in crowded but insecure conditions where survival was dependent on the constant maintenance of the dikes and waterworks.

The Trinh expanded southwards but failed to maintain the unity of Vietnam – unsurprisingly, given the geography of the country, which stretches for hundreds of kilometres along a mountain chain. After assuming power, the Trinh had maintained the fiction that the Le dynasty still controlled Dai Viet, and continued to do so even when the realm split in two. A second Vietnam grew up at the expense of the Chams and the north. A general of the Trinh, Nguyen Hoang, established in 1558 a military-based settlement in newly conquered territory to the south. For a time, he and his family acted as vassals of the Trinh, and they continued to recognize the Le as emperors, but in 1687 they overcame Trinh opposition and established a new, Nguyen capital at Hue. Southward expansion continued until the early nineteenth century. By the end of the seventeenth century, Vietnam claimed almost all of Champa, but a small area retained some freedom as a tributary state into the

The 'Le dynasty' ruler of Vietnam being carried in state, accompanied by his elephant and bearers of his parasols and fans, and followed by his mandarins. By the eighteenth century, when this drawing was made, the Le dynasty was a fiction. Vietnam was divided between the Trinh in the north and the Nguyen in the south.

nineteenth century. Many Cham survived in Vietnam, and even more in neighbouring Cambodia.

The south had many characteristics of pioneering regions: ample land (in contrast to the cramped situation in the north), open villages that were not surrounded by walls or hedges, an ethnically mixed population, and a lack of binding social institutions. It was, like other frontiers, a haven for rebels, criminals and exiles. Yet its plenitude of resources could not fail to attract the adventurous. As one folksong described it,

Birds fly to their hearts' content across the fields,
Fish race in droves in the immense sea and lakes.

Consolidating their new territories, Nguyen rulers became patrons of Mahayana Buddhism, under which they could subsume the local belief systems of both immigrants and Chams (although by the seventeenth century most Chams adhered to Islam). Sometimes, a traditional Cham deity was officially elevated to the Vietnamese pantheon. The Nguyen rulers welcomed Chinese immigrants (so-called 'Ming loyalists' fleeing the change of dynasty in China in 1644). Foreign trade flourished at the international emporium of Hoi An (Faifo); Japanese, Chinese, other Southeast Asians, Portuguese and Dutch did business there in the seventeenth and eighteenth centuries. With southern expansion, the Vietnamese found them-selves facing another neighbour, the Khmers, whose territory they also began to incorporate, finally establishing control of the Mekong Delta in the 1780s. The Nguyen territories were multi-ethnic, extending also to mountain peoples who supplied valuable forest products in exchange for salt and other goods. These upland commodities reached the coast through local markets. They were traded to foreign merchants at emporia like Hoi An.

In 1771–1802 the rebellion of the three Tayson brothers, named for their home village in south central Vietnam, put an end to Nguyen dominance in the south and wiped out the rule of the Trinh in the north as well. The rebellion is usually described as a peasant uprising, but a recent work has ascribed the unrest to problems with the hill peoples, who suffered from the collapse of international trade, debasement of coinage, and excessive taxation under late Nguyen rule. Whatever its origin, the rebellion rendered the Nguyen helpless. The last heir to the throne, Nguyen Anh, found refuge in Bangkok. There he received aid from Rama I that helped him return and ascend the throne of a united Vietnam as the Gia Long Emperor

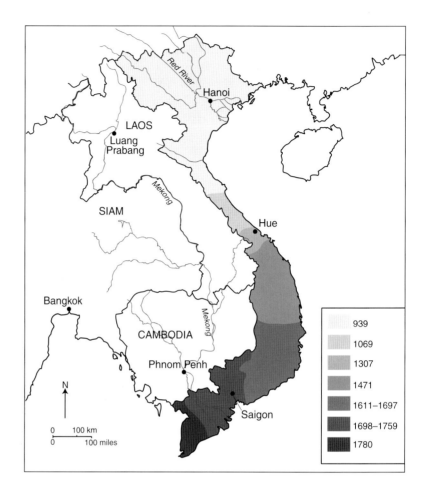

(r. 1802–20), with Hue as his capital. French merchants and
missionaries also supported his efforts.

The restored Nguyen dynasty needed to prove its legitimacy to
a populace devastated by rebellion and civil war; its means was the
propagation of Confucian orthodoxy. Gia Long, eager to limit the
competing influence of Buddhism, forbade adult men to attend
Buddhist ceremonies. His successor Minh Mang (r. 1820–41) placed
even more stress on Confucian orthodoxy, restricting Buddhism
and insisting that all monks be assigned to cloisters and carry
identification documents. He limited printed matter in general and
began a persecution of Catholic missionaries and converts that his
successors (not without provocation) continued. The fate of the
Christians attracted the attention of the French at a time of colonial
expansion, a tale continued below (see p. 106).

The restored monarchs vied with the Chinese emperors themselves in their adherence to Confucian orthodoxy. Yet even elite Vietnamese culture expressed other values. Vietnamese had borrowed Chinese words and used Chinese characters for writing, but they also developed and used *nom*, a system of writing with new characters to express uniquely Vietnamese terms. Society, culture and politics remained distinctive, incorporating indigenous Southeast Asian and Chinese elements.

## EUROPEAN CONTACTS AND EARLY COLONIZATION

No other Southeast Asian state had such an intensive exchange with China, but all of them would come under strong Western influences. When the first Europeans arrived in Southeast Asia in the sixteenth century they concentrated their attention on the maritime region, with its plethora of Islamic sultanates and other small kingdoms, the most important of which was the Sultanate of Malacca. After the fall of Malacca in 1511 to Portugal, other states such as Aceh in Sumatra and Johor on the Malayan Peninsula competed with Malacca for regional power. In westernmost Java, the Sultanate of Banten became a major port in the sixteenth century.

Many factors motivated the earliest European expansion into Southeast Asia. One was the search for spices for the European market. The second was the desire to participate in the trade in luxury goods with China, if necessary through Southeast Asia, where trade was possible even if China was closed to outsiders. In addition,

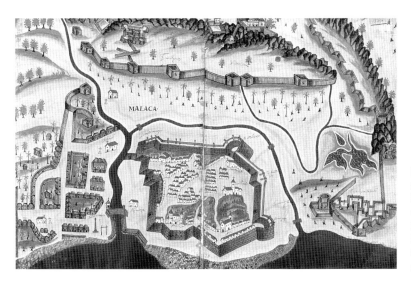

Malacca, in a map drawn shortly after the establishment of Portuguese rule in 1511. A wall encloses the European settlement. Portugal failed to maintain Malacca's dominant position in Southeast Asian trade, and other centres came to the fore.

Chinese silk was a luxury item of trade, reserved for Southeast Asian rulers and their close associates; it was also exported to Europe. In this early twentieth-century photograph, a queen and a princess of Laos display their richly woven and ornamented silk garments.

both Portuguese and Spanish vessels carried Catholic missionaries to the region, in the hopes of bringing Christianity to the furthest reaches of Asia.

Portugal arrived on the scene at the beginning of the sixteenth century. Its subjection of the Sultanate of Malacca provided it with a trading base on the Straits of Malacca. From there it extended its rule to the Spice Islands in eastern Indonesia (the Moluccas or Maluku), at that time the only place in the world where cloves, nutmeg and mace grew.

Portuguese ascendency, however, was short-lived. Corruption, cruelty and incompetence wore out its acceptance. Neighbouring Islamic sultanates attacked Malacca and tried to force the Christian intruders from the scene. Competition from the Dutch, who saw the Portuguese as rivals in politics, trade and religion, soon reduced Portugal's hold on its outposts in the maritime region. Forced from the Spice Islands in 1605, the Portuguese also had to concede Malacca to the Dutch in 1641. This ended Portugal's role in the maritime world; only part of the tiny island of Timor remained under Portuguese rule.

Spain profited from Ferdinand Magellan's realization that ships could reach Asia by sailing west as well as east. This navigator, originally from Portugal, brought his fleet to the Philippine Islands in 1521, claiming them for the Spanish king, but losing his life in an altercation with natives. Two decades later, the islands received the name of Philippines in honour of Philip II of Spain, and in the 1560s, colonization began in earnest. A major goal was the Christianization of the inhabitants. Except for the coast of the large southern island Mindanao and the islands of the Sulu Archipelago, Islam had not significantly penetrated the Philippines, although Manila was ruled by a Muslim when the Spanish arrived. 'States' hardly existed; native government and the economy functioned at the local level only.

Spain was not much interested in the produce of the islands; instead, it instituted a system of galleon trade, centred on the capital city, Manila, with its excellent harbour. Chinese junks arrived annually to offer silk and other fine goods to Spanish buyers. They accepted only silver in payment, so each year a galleon loaded with silver from the mines of Latin America would leave Acapulco for the islands, returning to Mexico with Chinese goods for Spain (nearly all contact with the motherland was via Mexico). This exchange dominated the colonial economy until 1815.

Manila had a small community of immigrant Chinese, who were usually temporary residents. Another group, Christianized descendants of Chinese fathers and native mothers grew up, called Chinese mestizos. The Spanish favoured the mestizos but were hostile to the immigrant Chinese who had not converted to Catholicism, and on several occasions attacked them violently. Both groups however continued to grow and the mestizos came to dominate the local economy. Political and ecclesiastical power remained firmly in the hands of Spain and its native-born, though the latter were a tiny minority. They manned a skeleton military and administrative staff in the colony.

The only officials in rural areas were the Spanish-born Catholic clergy, who were charged with converting the natives, providing them with some education where feasible, and integrating them as far as possible as subjects of Spain. A grateful motherland rewarded the religious orders who provided this backbone of the colony with extensive agricultural lands, which were often let out, under the control of managers, to small farmers. This made the Church largely self-supporting, while the expenses of administering Manila were met, in theory at least, by the profits from the galleon trade. In practice, illicit diversion of funds and profits for personal use left the public purse in debt. Exploitation of the colony for the world market by producing cash crops only began in the nineteenth century.

## COLONIZATION BY TRADE: THE VOC

While Spanish and Portuguese colonialism were ventures of the respective crowns, the Dutch colonized the Archipelago through the medium of a joint-stock company established in 1602, the United (Netherlands) East India Company or VOC (Vereenigde Oost-Indische Compagnie). (As late as the twentieth century, village people in the Indies still referred to the colonial government as *kumpeni*, 'the Company'.) This and other companies from European nations (an English East India Company was founded in 1600) existed for trade and profit rather than conquest. The first Dutch ships had arrived in the western Java harbour of Banten in 1596, where the sultan welcomed traders of all nations. Quarrelling with Banten, and reorganizing into the VOC, the Dutch moved to the north coast of

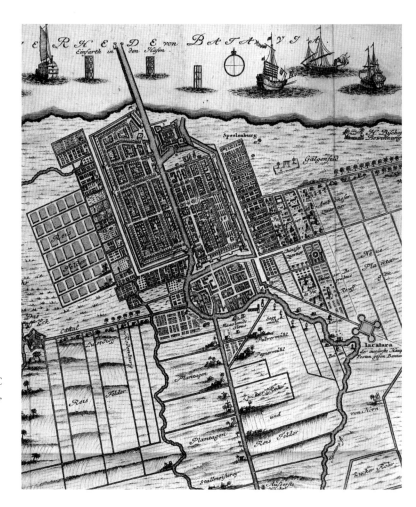

The city of Batavia in the seventeenth century. Europeans settled in the vicinity of the VOC fort, depicted in the upper centre, close to the harbour. Around the city were extensive rice and sugar-cane fields and Chinese market gardens. Remembering Amsterdam, the Dutch laid out canals for drainage and transportation.

Java, where they could better maintain contact with the Spice Islands and participate in other Asian trade. In 1619, the VOC's director in the Indies, Governor-General Jan Pieterzoon Coen, established the city of Batavia on the site of an earlier settlement called Jayakatra (now Jakarta). Batavia was an excellent base for the spice trade, which the Dutch now monopolized, and also attracted Chinese junks and native traders, becoming a real emporium of Asian trade. Over-coming rivalry with Banten and an attack by Sultan Agung of the central Javanese kingdom of Mataram in 1628–29, Batavia confirmed its place as headquarters of the VOC in Southeast Asia.

The Company was not interested in Christianization. In practice, Asian religions were widely tolerated and Islam grew in influence despite the Dutch presence. Nor did the VOC desire territorial aggrandizement because managing and defending large territories would divert profits to administrative expenses. What the VOC sought was trading points, either its own or at the headquarters of local rulers. It also wanted a monopoly in the products it traded, and so to exclude other traders, be they European or Asian, from dealing in the most desirable goods. Its ships carried heavy arms to enforce this exclusivity. Monopolizing the trade in spices was fairly simple, given that cloves and nutmeg only grew in a limited area, but in spite of its policy, VOC activities and weapons before long involved it in both territorial disputes and administrative expenses.

Batavia grew rapidly in importance. Many Chinese junks visited the port, exchanging Chinese products for regional goods. The VOC, unlike the Spanish, was well-enough equipped with trading vessels to make available Asian products that were in demand in China and to encourage their exchange in Batavia. Furthermore, many Chinese settled in the town, encouraged by the Dutch. Not only did Chinese provide labour for loading and unloading ships, but they built the canals, houses and much of the infrastructure of the town. Settlements of Chinese farmers soon surrounded the city. They grew vegetables for the tables of the VOC; sugar cane, from which they sometimes brewed arrack; and indigo, which they used for dyeing textiles in a process described by Denys Lombard as 'industrial agriculture *avant la lettre*'. Relations deteriorated, however. A threatened rebellion of Chinese immigrants in 1740 led the Dutch to clear the walled city of Chinese by means of a brutal massacre. Laws subsequently required Chinese to live in special sections of the towns under their own headman or *kapitan* (captain). Some areas of modern Jakarta, especially the northern part of the city, still seem like 'Chinatowns', although the typical Chinese shophouses have now nearly all disappeared, thanks both to urban development and, in 1998, a terrible riot which destroyed much of the traditional Chinese business district of Glodok.

Most of the rest of the population of Batavia was a mixture of immigrants from seafaring regions of the Indies and slaves from non-Islamic regions like Bali. The environs of the city were sparsely populated; Javanese and Sundanese (people from western Java), even Javanese slaves, were not allowed within the city walls for security reasons. Native settlement later increased, but for its first centuries, Batavia was a Chinese and Dutch city grafted onto a Javanese-Sundanese hinterland. Mestizo groups were strong, including Eurasians and Portuguese-speaking Christians; Batavia even had a Portuguese church. Only since Indonesian independence have the Javanese become a dominant group in the town, while ethnic Chinese form about ten per cent of contemporary Jakarta's inhabitants.

Another feature of the city was its prominent European or Eurasian families. The numbers of pure Dutch were small in early times, but men married local women – the Company required the ladies to become Christians – and founded local families. Batavia's women of the seventeenth and eighteenth centuries were a colourful contrast to their sombre sisters in the Netherlands. They loved elegant dress, they collected and displayed jewellery. Trying to behave as Europeans in public, they behaved in private as Southeast Asians. Slaves tended to their needs, especially betel-chewing. They bore Dutch names but they were more 'native' than 'Dutch'. Widowed husbands and, above all, sons might return to the Netherlands, but daughters would remain in the colony. Some local women founded major matrilineal families based in the colony, outliving their

A seventeenth-century visitor sketched these Batavian women enjoying a massage from their slaves.

husbands and using their inherited or earned fortunes to marry and remarry well, or to make good matches for their daughters.

Society in both Manila and Batavia, despite differences, retained a mestizo character into the nineteenth century. Only later did what J.S. Furnivall called 'plural societies' develop in the colonies, with a small European administrative and economic elite at the top of the pyramid, a large middle group of Chinese or other Asian immigrants in an intermediate economic position, and vast numbers of natives at the base, all of them meeting, so Furnivall wrote, only in the market-place. This description of racially ordered and divided societies became appropriate only in the more race-conscious twentieth century; in the Philippines, it probably never applied.

The Dutch planned Batavia, as the Spanish constructed Manila, on a European model. Batavia would have canals, as did Dutch cities. Soon its buildings were not of bamboo and thatch, like Southeast Asian dwellings, but of bricks and tile. The town hall, completed in 1710, is a typically Dutch construction. Northern European architecture was not entirely appropriate for tropical conditions, however, and the Dutch later adopted architecture better suited to the environment. By the nineteenth century, Batavia was expanding inland, and new urban areas were added in the twentieth century

Early Dutch colonial architecture followed models from the homeland, as this view of the old governor's palace in Batavia shows. Interiors were dark, stuffy and not very healthy. Mosquitoes multiplied in the swampy atmosphere and crocodiles occasionally took advantage of the canals.

further to the south. Jakarta today is a mega-city, reaching for dozens of kilometres into the countryside and harbouring densely-settled slum areas for its more than seven-million-strong population.

While the Spanish avoided close cooperation with the Chinese immigrants where they could (and on occasion murdered them), the Dutch found many uses for them as VOC authority expanded. Chinese were in the eighteenth and nineteenth centuries a source of revenue through poll taxes and taxes on items they consumed. They were useful as revenue farmers too: the Company 'farmed out' tolls, harbour duties and other taxes to Chinese who collected them and (usually) turned over a pre-agreed sum to the authorities. The Dutch were not the only colonial rulers to resort to these methods; later French and British governments, and the Siamese, too, used Chinese opium, gambling and alcohol 'farmers' to collect taxes on official monopolies. Revenue farming was a source of wealth, and those who had to bear its burden grew to resent it strongly.

## DUTCH TERRITORIAL CONQUESTS IN JAVA

The VOC had early occupied the Spice Islands. In addition to Batavia, it began to set up other bases in the Archipelago. It needed to provision its ships and its settlements with rice and other products from the countryside, and soon developed a voracious appetite for lumber from Java's teak forests, which was used for building and repairing ships. These interests brought the Company into conflict with the Sultanate of Mataram, based in central Java, which itself was in the process of trying to extend its rule to the independent coastal principalities along Java's north coast that had developed after the fall of Majapahit. Conflicts during the eighteenth century gave the Dutch more and more territorial control at the expense of Mataram.

Outside of Java, the Dutch usually were satisfied with establishing a trading post at a major port and trying to avoid further entanglement. This was not always successful, but the Dutch had few such bases and even fewer territories outside Java until after the Napoleonic Wars.

## THE EXPANSION OF EUROPEAN CONTROL

Western advances were not just achieved through superior firepower. However clever European weapons, Southeast Asians were just as clever in copying them. Burmese and Vietnamese kings fought wars with Portuguese guns. But the organization of most Southeast Asian states was weak: armies were unprofessional and not regularly drilled and disciplined. They were recruited from the countryside, preferably during the agricultural off-season, and easily deserted to their villages. Rulers frequently asked for European military assistance, since a few disciplined troops could create a considerable advantage in a local struggle for power. The VOC was most adept at this kind of service. In payment the Europeans often asked for – or took – new territories. The rulers' lack of attention to borders, lack of clear succession, and dispersion of authority among subordinates all gave Europeans a chance to intervene and gain at their expense. In the nineteenth century, presumed offences and pretexts for intervention were more and more common, and territorial conquest was finally justified by the supposed necessity of preventing other colonial powers from gaining a foothold.

As long as European colonies were urban enclaves, social change was limited and old traditions of authority remained in the country-side. Yet even early colonialism affected trading patterns, producing new wealth in some areas, and spreading poverty in others. A striking example is the deliberate destruction of the spice trees in the Spice Islands in the eighteenth century by the Dutch, who were convinced that oversupply was depressing the prices for cloves and nutmeg. The measure condemned the area to chronic poverty.

The territorial expansion of the VOC on Java finally eliminated Mataram, leaving two rival claimants to its heritage on Java, each with tiny territories, the Sultan of Yogyakarta and the Susuhunan of Surakarta. Yet the late eighteenth century saw the downfall of the VOC. Other traders were now active in the region, undermining the monopolies so important to the Company's hegemony. In 1786 the founding of the island of Penang as a British station off the west coast of the Malayan Peninsula gave British traders an additional advantage. The British, many of whom were private traders not associated with the East India Company, demanded free access to trade in the Archipelago and the Peninsula, and were now strong enough to undermine Dutch connections by dealing directly with local rulers. This rivalry cost the VOC dearly.

Other problems were internal. VOC officials were filling their own pockets first, and corruption contributed to the bankruptcy of the firm. Weighed down by debt, the VOC was abolished on 31 December 1799, and the Dutch state assumed its liabilities and its assets – one of which was most of the island of Java. In the following century, the Netherlands would extend territorial rule over the Indonesian Archipelago.

Singapore seen from Government Hill in 1830, just eleven years after it was founded by Sir Thomas Stamford Raffles (1781–1826). Raffles *(below)* had a keen intelligence and an enormous appetite for work. He assembled large collections on the nature, history and culture of Java and Sumatra.

## BRITAIN

The East India Company soon expanded from Penang Island to a strip of land on the Malayan Peninsula. During the Napoleonic Wars the British occupied Dutch possessions in Asia. In 1811, Thomas Stamford Raffles, an employee of the East India Company, became Lieutenant Governor of Java. After the British decided to return the Archipelago to the Dutch, Raffles founded a base in Singapore in 1819. This small village on an island at the tip of the Malayan Peninsula had an excellent harbour and was exceptionally well-suited to attract trade and to serve as an entrepôt for Southeast Asian products. Singapore grew rapidly, drawing thousands of Chinese and other immigrants, and becoming a base for Chinese as well as British economic interests in the region.

In 1824, the British and Dutch signed a treaty separating their interests in Southeast Asia. The British evacuated Benkulen in Sumatra, long a colony of the East India Company, while the Dutch turned over Malacca, now a second-rank harbour, to the British. The three British settlements of Penang, Singapore and Malacca became the Straits Settlements in 1826; they were transferred to the Colonial Office in 1867. At first, the British avoided further involvement on the Malayan Peninsula, but in the course of the nineteenth century, they built up a colony out of the diverse Malay

British troops storm the main stockade in Rangoon during the First Burma War of 1824–25. They consolidated their control over Burmese territory in two further wars of 1852 and 1885, making Rangoon their capital.

sultanates. Large-scale fighting during the 1860s and 1870s among Chinese tin miners working in the western Peninsula brought the British to intervene, then to consolidate their interests. In 1909, four northern Malay states that had been tributary to Siam – Kedah, Perlis, Kelantan and Trengganu – were added to the Malayan colonies.

A sideshow was the expansion of British interests into Borneo. The VOC had had various posts on Borneo in the eighteenth century but abandoned most of them before its dissolution. Nevertheless, the Dutch still thought this enormous island was securely within their sphere of interest when a British adventurer, James Brooke, established an independent state in Sarawak, adopting the Malay title of *raja* (king) in 1841. The Dutch promptly moved to secure their claims to the rest of Borneo. Sarawak, however, remained a Brooke-family-run kingdom until World War II, while in North Borneo, an independent British joint-stock company established control over a territory of its own. Both these states became member-states of Malaysia in 1963. The Sultanate of Brunei, to which much of northern Borneo was once tributary and which gave the island its name, became a British protectorate, and has since 1984 been an independent Islamic sultanate.

British interests in Burma were an extension of its India policy. Since Burma was adjacent to India, the first priority was to maintain security of the border. Burma failed to respond in a way the British felt they could trust; its rulers, the Konbaung dynasty, with their capital again at Ava, had a characteristically Southeast Asian lack of interest in borders. In 1824–25, the First Burma War resulted in the loss of the peripheral Burmese provinces of Arakan and Tenasserim to the British. A second war, in 1852, to punish the king's 'arrogance', secured British control of Lower Burma. The king retreated to Upper Burma, the core area of his realm. This more arid rump territory was not viable; famine ensued, and the opening of new land in the delta of Lower Burma attracted thousands of refugees and immigrants to British territory. A third war followed in 1885, partly to deter French expansion from Indochina that threatened India's flank. With the conquest of the capital at Mandalay, the Burmese monarchy was abolished and the land ruled directly as a part of the colony of India.

## FRENCH INDOCHINA

French interest in Indochina, as they later called it, was not only awakened by persecution of Catholics (see pp. 94–95), but also by the wish to secure the economic benefits of colonialism. In 1858–62, the French conquered the lower part of Vietnam, which they called Cochin China. This rather sparsely settled area offered possibilities for plantations and other commercial interests. The French subsequently extended their rule over the central part of the country around Hue, adopting the name Annam for this region, and, after a short period of fighting, took Hanoi in 1883, calling the north Tonkin. The name 'Vietnam' disappeared from official use. These three discrete colonies were finally combined with Cambodia (a protectorate since 1863) and Laos (most of which was subjected in 1893) into French Indochina. An emperor was retained in Hue, but his authority did not extend to Cochin China, which was directly ruled by France, and even in the protectorates of Annam and Tonkin French officials gave the orders. In 1907, the French ousted the Siamese from two formerly Cambodian provinces. In both Cambodia and Laos, kings remained in office, although the French now had a decisive voice in determining the succession to the throne. The Cambodian monarchy, at least, appeared grateful for French intervention, since that land had borne the brunt of both Vietnamese and Siamese aggrandizement for centuries, and Cambodians had reason to believe their territory would finally be swallowed by one or the other.

A French woman in nineteenth-century Indochina poses in a rickshaw. This two-wheeled vehicle was introduced into British and French dominions from Japan. Rickshaw pullers were among the poorest and most miserable of urban coolies.

King Sisowath of Cambodia (r. 1904–27, second from left) was dominated by French colonial administrators in the early decades of the twentieth century, as this line-up suggests. The French gold braid and sash, however, are barely a match for the silks and satins of the Khmer court

## USA

One more country would join the ranks of the Southeast Asian colonial powers in 1898, when the USA acquired the Philippines from Spain after a short war over their respective interests in the Caribbean. The declared intention of the American colonial experiment, against considerable domestic opposition, was, in the word of President William McKinley, to 'Christianize' the population – some two hundred years after Spain had accomplished the task.

## CONSOLIDATION OF INDEPENDENCE IN SIAM

Only Siam escaped colonization. By the early twentieth century, although much reduced in territory, it remained an independent state, and was at least freed of its rivalry with Burma. The successors of King Rama I (r. 1782–1809) changed Siam from a mandala-state – one in which the centre exercised loose control over satellite polities and territory expanded or contracted according to the strength of alliances with those satellites – to a modern, territorially defined state. By the time of Mongkut (Rama IV, r. 1851–68), the Siamese recognized the dangers of European colonialism and resorted to a careful programme of change to meet the colonial challenge. Successive kings integrated subordinate polities, though they subsequently lost some of them to British and French expansion on the mainland. On the other hand, modernization (sometimes with the help of foreign advisors) and diplomacy enabled Siam to retain its political independence.

King Chulalongkorn (Rama V) of Siam poses with his son, the crown prince. Chulalongkorn combined a brilliant mind with both Western and Asian education and instituted major reforms in Siam's society and government.

Mongkut and his gifted son Chulalongkorn (Rama V, r. 1868–1910) deserve much of the credit for this. They also helped Siam's cause when they convinced the British that it would be in their interest to preserve Siam's independence and to keep the French at bay. Their successors were less adept, and changes in Siamese society brought new groups to the fore. In 1932, new civilian and military elites forced the reigning king, Prajadhipok (Rama VII, r. 1925–35), to accept a constitution, ending Siam's absolute monarchy.

## CHAPTER FIVE

# New Directions, New Elites
## *The Colonial Map of Southeast Asia*

The nineteenth century brought a new kind of colonialism. The major colonial powers – Britain, the Netherlands, France, Spain, the USA – were filling out the map of Southeast Asia in their own colours. Various factors led to intervention: internal disputes in still-independent kingdoms; the desire to put a stop to piracy, slave-trading or opium smuggling; petty attacks on existing colonies; or simply a grab for potential natural resources, land and minerals. Only Siam managed to fend off colonization, but it underwent many of the economic changes that the rest of the region did.

Colonialism was now a state enterprise. The Dutch East India Company (the VOC) was dissolved, bankrupt, at the dawn of the nineteenth century, and the British East India Company followed some decades later. Colonial policy became an issue for parliaments and the metropolitan press. Southeast Asians were now beginning to rebel against the effects of foreign rule, at first in traditional ways, then gradually finding a voice in national movements, with their own press and literature and their own leaders. Increasingly they were conscious of themselves as members of territorially defined nations, and not merely of families, villages or ethnic groups. Challenging the rationale for colonial rule, in some ways they were the children of colonialism itself.

The territorial impact of the new colonialism is easy to illustrate. In 1800 the possessions of the Dutch East India Company in Indonesia were limited to Java, the Spice Islands, and a few stations through the Archipelago. In 1910, the Netherlands East Indies was virtually co-extensive with the Archipelago; only northern Borneo

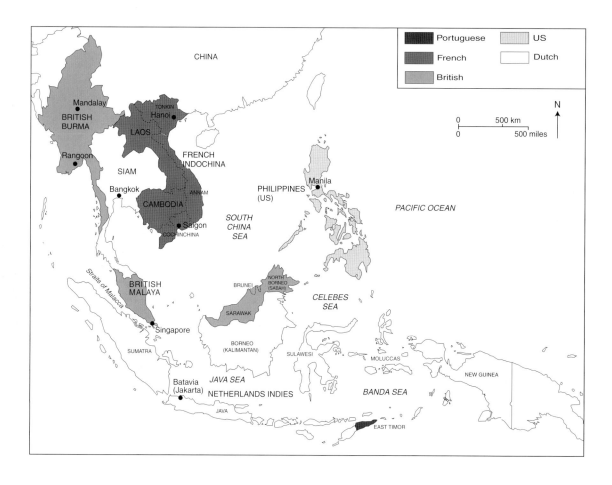

Southeast Asia under colonial domination in the early twentieth century.

and Portuguese East Timor were not part of the colony. New Guinea was divided. Britain in 1800 had a station in Penang, but not even an outpost in Burma. The only contact the French had with the Indochina states was through missionaries or traders. The Philippines were already a Spanish colony, but the southern part, where inhabitants adhered to Islam, still resisted Spanish rule. Soon after 1900, there was nothing left to colonize, Britain and France having agreed to maintain Siam as an independent buffer between their domains.

This listing fails to illustrate the economic and psychological impact of colonialism. Western powers brought to bear the entire weight of their rapidly developing technology and industry for both peaceful and belligerent purposes: road-building, telecommunications, printing presses, modern weapons, railroads, automobiles, steamships, electricity. The devices and infrastructure established by Westerners in order better to exploit the resources of the colonies themselves laid the foundations of new national awareness.

By the early twentieth century, Western schools were opening more widely, most teaching the same curriculum used in the metropoles. Often the schools were run by Christian missionaries, who were confident that their pupils could and would adopt their mores. Whereas previously the European colonists had largely been single men who adapted their lifestyle to the surroundings, now entire families came to live, confronting tropical habits with Western ways. Finally, Western-owned enterprises, mines and plantations were expanding and beginning to employ a sizeable Asian labour force.

In a coffee plantation in Java in the nineteenth century, barefoot labourers rake and dry the beans while the European owner or manager, hand on hip, keeps a watchful eye on their activities.

## AGRICULTURAL CHANGE AND POPULATION GROWTH

The economic and political thrust of colonialism set the stage for wide-ranging changes in population and agriculture. Robert Elson has called the period beginning in about 1800 Southeast Asia's 'Age of the Peasant'. In less than one and a half centuries, peasants transformed and intensified their farming methods, adapted new crops, and became producers for world markets. Still remaining tied to villages and, for the most part, to subsistence production, they nevertheless forged contacts with the wider economy, something that brought them both profit and economic distress.

Southeast Asian peasants also opened new lands, a process which went hand-in-hand with population growth. At the beginning of the nineteenth century, forest covered most of Southeast Asia and even much of Java was densely wooded; by 1945, little forest was left in Java, and elsewhere it had receded significantly. In Thailand, Vietnam's Mekong Delta, and Lower Burma, movements of people resulted in the draining of previously uninhabited wetlands for rice agriculture. In areas that were already populated, irrigation was extended and refined, and the double-cropping of rice became more common.

In uplands, dry field or swidden farming (see p. 35) was widely replaced by more productive but more labour-intensive cultivation. In some hill regions, population growth put such pressure on 'nomadic' swidden farmers that many changed to sedentary agriculture, even planting wet rice. Most governments supported this transition, not only because they regarded shifting cultivation as ecologically destructive but because they also wanted their subjects to settle and be available for tax collections or corvée. In some cases, as after the Java War, which pitted Prince Diponegoro against the colonialists in a dogged fight lasting from 1825 to 1830, or after a smaller rebellion on the island of Bangka that interfered with tin production between 1850 and 1851, the Dutch forced rural inhabitants to settle in well-defined villages for security reasons, a policy the British would apply in Malaya in the 1950s.

Shifting cultivators did not disappear entirely, but they were pushed to the fringes of settlement. Some of these groups responded by introducing the planting of tree crops for export, particularly, in the twentieth century, rubber. Rubber was easy to integrate into their usual pattern of work since the trees, once planted, needed little care. Swidden agriculture demanded considerable labour input at times of clearing, planting and harvesting. Rubber trees could be tapped and the rubber sold for cash income at times when there were few other demands on labour. In the Netherlands Indies, rubber smallholders produced almost as much rubber for export as the large Western-owned plantations, though they could not match their quality. In times of growing demand, as in the 1920s, rubber and other export crops could provide a good cash income.

The trend to cash cropping did not stop at upland farmers. Rice itself grew to be the most important export crop in Burma, Thailand and southern Vietnam in the second half of the nineteenth century. Growers found a market in rice-deficient areas of the region: in the cities, in northern Vietnam, India and China, and in the plantations and mines, with their tens of thousands of coolies.

In the older colonies of Java and the Philippines, colonial powers had at first attempted to force villagers to produce crops for the world market in addition to the rice they grew for their own consumption. From 1830 to about 1870, a system of compulsory cultivation of sugar, indigo, coffee and other exportable products was in force in Java. After the abolition of this 'Cultivation System' – partly because of public criticism of its handling of the natives, partly because commercial interests were pushing for liberalization of trade and investment – privately-owned sugar mills began to be established in

Javanese women transplant rice seedlings into a flooded field. This method increases harvests but requires hours of back-breaking labour.

rural areas. Sugar was grown in rotation with rice on peasant plots and processed in these new, mechanical mills, which were owned by Western or Chinese firms. Economic historians believe that large-scale sugar growing and processing opened new opportunities for employment, especially for those with little land, but the system remained unpopular with villagers. When the Indonesian Revolution broke out in 1945, the sugar mills were the first target of the nationalists' scorched-earth strategy.

In the Philippines the Spanish required peasants to grow tobacco for local and international consumption – Manila cigars were a product of this system. Sugar production expanded in areas like the central Philippine islands of Negros and Iloilo. Under American rule, Philippine sugar enjoyed a highly rewarding, protected export market in the USA, although rewards inevitably fell more to landowners and millers than to farmers.

Rapid expansion of agricultural output required capital. A major input was the labour of the peasants themselves since they felled the trees, drained swamps and built irrigation systems. In some cases,

Western capital supported the intensification or expansion of native agriculture; in Java, for example, colonial and private interests contributed to the construction of irrigation works that enabled the profitable symbiosis of rice and sugar cane cultivation.

Rural areas had no functioning credit associations before the 1920s or so, and those later founded did not work well. Many peasants borrowed cash from well-to-do villagers. A major source of credit was the Indian and Chinese immigrants who toured the villages, lending small amounts for agricultural use or for expenses like weddings and funerals. Immigrant Chettiars, a South Indian moneylending caste, helped finance agriculture in Lower Burma and to a lesser extent in southern Vietnam and the Malayan Peninsula. Another group were the itinerant Chinese peddlers who brought consumer goods and agricultural necessities into the villages, selling them on credit or, like their Indian counterparts, offering loans.

This amiable Chinese gentleman earned his living in Java as an itinerant peddler, carrying his miscellaneous goods in a bundle. He shakes a rattle to attract customers.

Chinese shopkeepers or traders were familiar figures in rural areas of Siam, the Philippines, much of Indonesia and southern Vietnam. As intermediate traders they also served an important function in gathering export crops for market. Chinese businessmen practically monopolized rice milling in southern Vietnam, exporting the product through Cholon, the Chinatown of Saigon.

Peasants did gain from the intensification of agriculture, but, in retrospect, these gains were precarious and uneven. In the Netherlands Indies, peasants could only lose their lands to creditors of local origin, since agrarian legislation prohibited ethnic Chinese from holding agricultural land. Instead growers mortgaged their unripe crops to the Chinese for less than market value. In Vietnam and the Philippines, on the other hand, many small farmers lost their property to large landholders and to Indian or Chinese moneylenders, especially in the 1930s when the Depression drove rice prices down and caused borrowers to default. By 1937, Indian Chettiars in Lower Burma had taken control of some 25 per cent of cropped land, which aroused Burman resentment against this group. The problem of unequal distribution of land became more acute everywhere as opportunities to pioneer new sites decreased and competition for available plots increased.

The problem was not entirely one of credit and default. Densely populated northern Vietnam, Java and parts of the Philippines were not producing enough rice to meet their needs.

Rapid population growth caused landholdings to be divided into ever smaller parcels; many villagers could not live from their shrinking plots. Traditional mechanisms for redistribution had guaranteed the poor a share in paid labour, the opportunity to rent land from larger landholders, use of communal village land, and small-scale aid from landlords in times of crisis. These practices fell into disuse as landlords moved to the cities, removing themselves from claims to redistribution of wealth; some landlords were outsiders. World War I and especially the Depression caused great distress in rural areas. Farmers substituted cassava or maize for rice to survive; smallholders who grew rubber and other export products often returned to subsistence crops when world markets collapsed. Toward the end of the 1930s, prior to the outbreak of World War II, prices for exports revived and production temporarily recovered.

## MINES, PLANTATIONS AND IMMIGRANT LABOUR

One motivation for nineteenth century colonial expansion was the search for natural resources. Western firms opened mines and agricultural plantations to meet the ever-increasing demands of the industrial nations for raw materials.

Many deposits of metals are found close to the surface in Southeast Asia, and early mining had entailed the extraction of metals by small groups working with the simplest tools. A belt of tin ore deposits reaches from China through Burma and Thailand down the Malayan Peninsula to the Indonesian islands of Bangka and Belitung; gold, iron and copper deposits were widely known. While Southeast Asian metalworking was highly skilled – as Dongson drums, metal gongs, and finely-worked swords and krisses testify – native mining was an almost desultory process, engaged in by people who also had other ways to make a living.

In the eighteenth century, local rulers invited Chinese labourers to mine gold and tin, often displacing natives from that activity. Chinese worked in larger groups, they had better ways of organizing and disciplining labour, and their superior, though still simple, technology enabled them to exploit deposits more efficiently. Other Chinese labourers worked the pepper and gambier plantations in the Riau Archipelago in the eighteenth century. Abandoning worked-over territory, they moved on to Singapore in the nineteenth century, then to Johor. Here, too, Chinese financed the enterprises, imported and controlled labour, and organized sales and exports, but the first impulse seems to have come from native rulers.

In the early twentieth century, Chinese still provided most of the skilled and unskilled labour in Southeast Asian cities. They worked this Western-owned gold mine in Sarawak *(left)* and a Singapore coal yard *(below)*. The gold mine's wooden wheel is a Chinese pump that had once removed water from the mine; by this date a steam locomotive provides energy to expel the water and lift out the ore.

Chinese tin miners in the Malayan Peninsula taking a break. They worked in shifts around the clock.

Apart from organization and technology, there was another reason to use immigrant labourers. With the exception of 'pockets' of dense population, such as in Java and northern Vietnam, Southeast Asia was a thinly populated region far into the nineteenth century. As a result, labour was scarce and expensive. So long as land was available and harvests were adequate, Southeast Asians did not need to work under the miserable conditions to which miners and plantation labourers were subjected. From about 1860, Western firms, now also beginning to enter mining and plantations, used Chinese, recruiting them on a temporary basis.

These labourers – coolies – were not free men. The costs of their passage and upkeep, purchases from the company store, tobacco, alcohol and opium were all charged to the workmen. When, at the end of their contract, they were unable to repay their debts with interest, they had to remain on the job. Those who tried to leave could be severely punished. A majority of coolies did return to their homelands, if not after their first term, then some time later. A lucky few might transfer some earnings to the homeland and restart life there, while some remained in the new lands, settling in as small farmers or traders, but very few achieved the transition from 'rags to riches' that so many immigrants dreamed of. At times twenty per cent or more died annually from diseases such as tuberculosis, cholera or beri-beri. In the Malayan Peninsula, in addition to immigrant Chinese, Indian and Sri Lanka Tamil labourers worked in the first rubber plantations and some found jobs in public employment or in building and maintaining the railroads.

An Indian woman labourer taps a rubber tree by cutting a strip of the bark. The sap – raw latex – runs into a cup and is collected daily and processed.

Floating tin dredges can work in flooded mine pits or at sea, where tin is found near river mouths. By performing all tasks from digging to cleaning and separating the ore, the dredges took much of the drudgery out of mining – which in turn ceased to be exclusively a task for Chinese coolies.

China deeply resented the coolie traffic, making recruitment difficult, and in time, as the prices for Chinese coolies rose, the import of Chinese labour became too expensive for local firms. As a result, the tobacco plantations of East Sumatra hired first men and then women from populous and increasingly impoverished areas of Java. By the 1920s, coolies from Java (many of them women) had displaced the Chinese from most plantation jobs. Small industries, rubber plantations, and coal mines in Vietnam found densely populated Tonkin in the north a ready source of workers. Many peasants resorted to what is now called 'circular migration', alternating between the village (at times of planting or harvesting) and the working-place. One observer in the mid-1930s estimated that two-thirds of the people of Tonkin engaged in work for wages during at least part of the year.

In the tin mines of Malaya, southern Thailand, Bangka and Belitung, local people refused to do the back-breaking labour of digging and carrying. But once large-scale machinery had eliminated drudgery and changed the nature of mining in the twentieth century, Malays and Indonesians replaced Chinese coolies (just as Western capitalists once replaced Chinese entrepreneurs), a transition completed after World War II. Unlike the mining of metals, the highly mechanized petroleum industry was always a Western endeavour.

The influx of foreign labour – even though only a minority of immigrants actually stayed – permanently changed the ethnic composition of some areas. Coolies accounted for only part of the immigration from China and India; others too came to all Southeast Asian countries to seek their fortune, especially in urban areas. In the twentieth century, women and children accompanied the immigrants. Malays became a minority in parts of the Peninsula; in East Sumatra, substantial Chinese and Javanese minorities formed, while by 1930 over forty per cent of the population of Bangka and Belitung were of Chinese origin. The city of Rangoon had an Indian majority in 1931. Singapore, a centre for coolie traffic, soon had a Chinese majority; today over three-quarters of its population is of Chinese origin.

During the Depression of the 1930s, mines and plantations fell into crisis. Thousands of coolies were discharged; those who did not return to their homelands often settled on nearby agricultural plots. The export economy, whether supplied by smallholders or Western-owned industries, partly recovered before the outbreak of World War II, but the era of coolie migration was at an end. Even today, however, villagers from densely-populated regions still migrate to cities and to less developed areas, a movement that has had devastating ecological consequences in some areas. Land-clearing, often by fire, has produced widespread, choking smogs, and denuding the soil has fostered erosion.

A young Chinese woman shopping in Singapore. In the nineteenth century, single men dominated most Chinese settlements abroad; in the twentieth century, increased immigration of women from China enabled the Chinese to form stable, more family-centred communities.

## EARLY RESISTANCE

Moves to consolidate colonial dominions took various forms. The Americans, having defeated the Philippine nationalist resistance, incorporated the Islamic minority in the south, the Moros, by means of war. The British concluded their expansion into Upper Burma in 1886 by deposing the monarch. In 1914 'British Malaya' consisted of the largely Chinese and urban Straits Settlements of Singapore, Penang and Malacca; the economically important Federated Malay States, whose rulers had, in the nineteenth century, agreed to accept the advice of British officials; and a third group, the Unfederated Malay States, which comprised Johor and four Malay sultanates wrested from Siamese hegemony. The Dutch filled out their map of

This photograph of Indonesian soldiers and their European officers illustrates the brutality of the colonial war in Aceh. The native soldiers were equipped with special uniforms and weapons and encouraged to show no pardon to the rebels, many of whom believed they were fighting an Islamic holy war.

the Netherlands Indies through successful wars against Lombok, Bali and Aceh, and persuaded other local rulers to submit to incorporation into the colony.

Early resistance to colonial expansion took different forms: millenarian movements and other religiously inspired opposition, restorationism, apparently spontaneous violence, or guerilla warfare. At first in the Philippines, then in Vietnam, anti-colonialism gradually began to emerge in the form of organized movements with explicit political and economic goals.

Sometimes resistance was stubborn and bloody. When the Dutch moved against the small kingdoms of southern Bali and of Lombok, their troops faced suicidal ritual confrontations (called *puputan* in Balinese) with the members of these courts, who deliberately put themselves and their families in the line of fire and drove krisses into their own hearts rather than face defeat. The stubbornest opposition came from Aceh at the northern tip of Sumatra, a region with a long Islamic tradition. In the 1870s, the Dutch found several reasons to take this once-proud sultanate. The area harboured pirates and threatened the security of the adjacent, rapidly developing plantation area of East Sumatra. Rumours circulated hinting at mineral wealth or that other powers were interested in the area. In 1874 colonial troops easily overran the capital and the court, but Islamic teachers soon took up the fight against the intruders, waging determined guerilla war and invoking the Muslim tradition of *jihad* or *perang sabil* (as Islamic holy war is called in Indonesia), with the promise of paradise for any who died at the enemy's hands. Dutch forces only pacified Aceh in 1913, and even then incidents continued. The Aceh War was history's longest colonial war, and one of the most bitter.

## THE BEGINNINGS OF NATIONALISM

In general, colonial authorities liked to work with traditional elites. Where these were willing to cooperate, they were rewarded with an enhancement of their position and responsible offices. (Those who were not willing to cooperate might lead rebellions, as did Prince Diponegoro in Java.) Many historians believe that this policy had a widespread and detrimental impact on the balance of power in indigenous societies, strengthening the position of the ruler against the aristocracy (as in Cambodia) or of the aristocracy against other elements in society (as in the Netherlands Indies). The Dutch in Java worked closely with the existing Javanese elite, the *priyayi*, opening positions in the bureaucracy to them. Collaborating mandarins in Vietnam became a backbone of French colonial rule.

The earliest nationalist movements of Southeast Asia were founded by Filipinos with advanced Western education, something that was only available much later in other colonies. Among the first Philippine nationalists were the native Catholic clergy. Educated to be priests, they were nevertheless denied entry into religious orders and had little opportunity to become pastors in their own parishes. Three native priests were executed for anti-Spanish sentiments in 1872, as was José Rizal, physician, novelist and nationalist, in 1896.

Still, many of the educated hesitated to break with Spain, leaving leadership of protest movements in other hands. When the Katipunan, a mass movement infused with unorthodox religious practices and led by Andres Bonifacio (1863–97), won over some young educated Filipinos (often called *ilustrados*) to the fight against Spanish rule, the Philippine anti-colonial revolution was born. The rebels proclaimed a republic on 12 June 1898, formulating a constitution in the following year. It would remain for the Americans, taking over the islands from Spain, to fight a drawn-out war to suppress the movement.

European colonial officials, like the local native elite, cherished a display of official regalia. In this portrait, the Dutch Resident of Semarang in central Java poses with his servant and his ceremonial parasol.

The American occupiers succeeded in winning over much of the educated and land-holding elite to cooperation by offering them administrative and political roles as early as 1900, and in 1916 by promising future independence. The decision to make peace with the new overlords paved the way for the elite's subsequent domination of Philippine politics. Other Filipinos resisted stubbornly until 1902, and in some places for years afterward.

In Vietnam a restorationist movement, Can Vuong (Loyalty to the King), combined elite leadership with mass expectations. It was founded in 1885, just after the French consolidated their rule throughout Vietnam. The heir-apparent to the Vietnamese throne, Ham Nghi, had fled the royal city of Hue, and the French enthroned his brother. Much of the scholar-gentry, however – the mandarins who were the backbone of the traditional state – chose loyalty to the exiled prince and to the precolonial order. Ham Nghi's capture in 1888 ended the immediate threat, but many mandarins remained unreconciled to the new rulers.

SOCIAL CHANGE: EDUCATION, LANGUAGE AND LITERACY

By the beginning of the twentieth century, Western schools were expanding rapidly in many colonies to meet the need for trained personnel. Native Southeast Asians were attending modern schools, but the colonial administrations, like the Spanish Philippine church before them, reserved senior positions for Europeans. Race-consciousness also grew as larger numbers of Westerners settled in the colonies.

Changes in the economy, however, did open posts for educated natives from outside the traditional elite. The expansion of government services made more positions available in the lower bureaucracy, in Western enterprises, and in schools, bringing new groups into direct contact with colonial hierarchies. Young people from small towns and rural areas moved to the capitals (or even to Western countries) to work and study, meeting others from distant regions with similar experiences. The awakening of national consciousness in the Philippines was repeated in other colonies. Labourers also became more aware of their interests, and the first unions formed.

These trends contributed to an emerging national awareness that was reinforced by modern communications: the printing press, steamships, telephone and telegraph. The growth of literacy in vernacular languages enabled the spread of new ideas. In the Philippines, Spanish and then English became a common language for the educated. In the Netherlands Indies, Malay, a lingua franca since the time of Malacca and Srivijaya, was the language of the colonial administration, the cities and the marketplace; only a few Western-educated spoke Dutch. Malay would become the Indonesian national language. From the late nineteenth century, a popular literature and press in Malay transmitted ideas of modernization, nationalism and emancipation. That only a minority were literate was no barrier to the popularity of this material: those who could, read aloud or retold the stories for those who could not. The indigenous press gave nationalism a voice, but official censorship still kept the expression of anti-colonial sentiments in check.

In 1905, the Netherlands Indies government elected to produce its own reading matter. This led to the foundation of Balai Pustaka, a government publishing and distribution firm that produced books and journals in Malay and vernacular languages. The intention was to provide schools and the reading public with 'appropriate' material – 'good reading matter from which at the same time we might expect a politically desirable influence', as an official explained. Many of Indonesia's best-known early writers were published by Balai Pustaka; a few were rejected for political or other reasons.

Vietnam witnessed a near-explosion of popular literature in the twentieth century. Some 10,000 titles – books and pamphlets – were published between 1923 and 1944, in addition to hundreds of periodicals. These texts appeared in *quoc-ngu*, in the Latin alphabet. Previously Vietnamese had been written with a variation of Chinese characters (*nom*), and the educated learned to read and write classical Chinese as well. *Quoc-ngu* was the script of the colonial power, but nationalists and writers soon turned it into a popular vehicle, not only for entertainment, but to discuss such issues of the day as the relation between tradition and modernity, ethics and politics, the importance of education, and the role of women. *Quoc-ngu* contributed to both more widespread literacy and understanding of the issues facing the nation.

## INTERNATIONAL INFLUENCES ON THE
## EMERGENCE OF NATIONALISM

Given the crossroads position of Southeast Asia, it is no surprise that nationalism in the region did not develop in isolation. The Meiji Revolution in Japan, beginning in 1868, raised the question of modernization of Asian countries, as the Japanese adopted education, law and technology from Western countries. In 1899, Japanese were accorded the legal status of 'European' in Netherlands Indies law, something which greatly offended the local Chinese minority (who were treated as 'natives' and yet were denied some native rights) and increased their awareness of being a disadvantaged minority despite belonging to the great Chinese nation. More dramatic was the Japanese victory over Russia in the war of 1904–05; this Asian victory over a Western power made a lasting impression on young nationalists everywhere in Southeast Asia.

The Chinese Revolution of Sun Yatsen in 1911, preceded by years of reform, attempted revolution and failures, also had reverberations further south. While its effect was most strongly felt in nearby Vietnam, it also touched Chinese populations outside China, especially those in Southeast Asia. Sun had spent years trying to mobilize Chinese in Southeast Asia for his campaign to abolish the Manchu emperors, whom he regarded as foreign occupiers, and to establish a Chinese republic. The reformer Kang Youwei, who had fled from China to Singapore in 1898, propagated Neo-Confucianist ideas. In 1899 Chinese in the Indies founded an association to 'purify' local customs – that is, to make them more Confucianist. They soon began to promote modern Chinese-language education. Within a few years the Chinese, now more nationally conscious than ever, had opened hundreds of modern, Mandarin-language schools in their communities. The example was not lost on the native public, who on the one hand tried to imitate Chinese organizations, while on the other organizing against the economic challenge posed by expanding Chinese-owned businesses.

Some nationalists in Burma looked to India, with its well-established national movement, as a model. The Russian Revolution of 1917 was another influence, in Burma and elsewhere. Within a few years, Communist parties appeared, first in the Indies and then further afield.

Finally, contacts with the Near East became much more frequent thanks to improved communications and steamship travel. More and more Muslims made the pilgrimage to Mecca, many remaining for years to study Islamic thought or to become initiated into one of the Islamic brotherhoods. Others chose to visit Islamic institutions of higher learning. The Al-Azhar University in Cairo was a favourite destination of young people who wanted to learn about politics as well as modernist Islam. These influences contributed to the founding of the Sarekat Islam (see p. 128).

## REFORM MOVEMENTS

Small-scale reformist movements dominated the early nationalism of the educated. In Indonesia, the administrative elite had expanded to include groups from the lesser elite, a new *priyayi* dominated by men who rose through education, not inheritance. It was some of these – students of the medical college in Batavia, at the time the only institution of higher education in the colony – who in 1908 formed Budi Utomo ('glorious endeavour'), the first Indonesian nationalist organization. Largely Javanese in membership, its primary goal was to 'uplift' the natives.

This was also the aim of R.A. Kartini (1879–1904), a young Javanese woman from the lesser nobility who in her letters to Dutch friends, published in 1911, expressed hope for enlightenment and, especially, for greater opportunities for women, inspiring others to follow her ideals: 'We have no right to be stupid.' These small beginnings, with their emphases on reform and cooperation with the colonial power, bore the seeds of a pan-Indonesian nationalism that would later reject European tutelage.

The rise of Japan and, more directly, the Chinese Revolution of 1911 were also an example to young Vietnamese intellectuals who surrounded the mandarin Phan Boi Chau (1867–1940), whose nationalist ideals were combined with a conservative social philosophy, and who contributed to violent if small-scale uprisings. His trial for conspiracy in 1925 touched off a series of public protests. A contemporary, Phan Chu Trinh (1872–1926), favoured non-violence and social reform, also attacking the oppressive mandarins who collaborated with French rule. Small-scale attacks on French power, including a mutiny of indigenous naval forces in Yen Bay in 1930 inspired by the Nationalist Party of Vietnam (named after the Nationalist Party of China), provoked brutal repression. A stubborn peasant rebellion in that year in Nghe An and Ha Tinh provinces, complete with organized 'soviets', pointed to the participation of Communists. In the end, however, Vietnamese nationalists were divided and, above all, outgunned.

## MARXISM

Influences from the metropoles contributed to the spread of Marxism. A representative of the Dutch Social Democratic Party living in the Netherlands Indies, together with several politically interested Javanese, founded the Indies Social Democratic Association in 1914. This would become the Communist Party of the Indies (established 1920) and later, that of Indonesia, known by its initials PKI. The party collaborated for a time with the Islamic mass movement, Sarekat Islam. In 1926 and 1927 in Banten (western Java) and in West Sumatra, PKI adherents staged an ill-planned uprising that provoked immediate colonial retaliation. Many of the hundreds arrested were exiled under dreadful conditions to the isolated camp of Boven Digul in West New Guinea. Only a tiny underground organization survived until World War II.

In 1920, Nguyen Ai Quoc (1890–1969), the pseudonym of the son of a disaffected Vietnamese mandarin, joined the Communist Party of France, attracted by its anti-colonialism. He had remained in France after World War I and spent much of the interwar period in exile there, in Russia and finally in China, where he took the name Ho Chi Minh. Ho founded the Indochinese Communist Party in 1930, bringing together several existing groups. Eleven years later, he would try to unite all Vietnamese nationalists in a League for the Independence of Vietnam, known by its abbreviated title Viet Minh. Until World War II there remained a number of competing nationalist organizations in Vietnam, even though the French managed to incarcerate or execute many of their supporters, but the Viet Minh eventually came to dominate the movement.

Communist movements in Siam and Malaya were still largely limited to the Chinese minority. The tiny Western-educated elite in Siam, linked to court, army and bureaucracy, was seldom open to Marxism. In what was then called British Malaya, the colonial power had kept the Malays a largely rural people. The Malay way of life had changed little, and radical ideas found scant reception among the native population. Instead, most remained loyal to their sultans, who cooperated with the British. Small socialist and Communist parties existed in the Philippines in the 1930s, although the latter was outlawed.

Nevertheless, Marxist ideas about imperialism were widely popular, penetrating many organizations that were not explicitly Communist. Many educated Southeast Asians thought that Marxism and socialism explained their own experience, pointing to the

*(Above)* The Indonesian Communist Party or PKI quickly won adherents in Java and parts of Sumatra after its founding in 1920. The officers of the Batavia branch of the party posed for this photograph in 1925.

*(Left)* Southeast Asia's best-known Marxist, Ho Chi Minh, photographed before World War II. Ho's name replaced an earlier revolutionary pseudonym, Nguyen Ai Quoc (Nguyen the Patriot).

dominance of Western capital in the colonies. Not surprisingly, therefore, socialism came to be part of the expressed policy of their governments after independence, and many governments subsequently enforced nationalization and state control of strategic sectors of the economy.

## RELIGION AND NATIONALISM

Probably the most potent ingredient of Southeast Asian anti-colonialism was religion. Bonifacio had appealed to native Philippine religious traditions (see p. 121), as did a young Filipino Catholic priest, Gregorio Aglipay. He rebelled against rigid colonial church structures and founded his own native church in 1902. Aglipay at one time had thousands of followers, but the majority deserted him when the Americans diffused the rebellion by restoring occupied churches to mainstream Catholicism, while at the same time instituting secular government and depriving the religious orders of their large landholdings, a major grievance against the Catholic Church.

Religion was also a means to shore up self-worth in the face of intruding Westernization and to unite natives against outsiders. Young Burmans in Rangoon responded to their colonial situation and to Christian missionary activity with a Young Men's Buddhist Association, founded in 1906. The unsuccessful Saya San Rebellion of 1930 displayed a mixture of millenarian and modern appeals. At the same time, Southeast Asian nationalists tried to incorporate modern developments like science, technology, socialism and mass literacy into their religious perspectives. This led some traditional Islamic schools, for example, to enlarge their curriculum to include modern subjects, just as the Chinese minorities had replaced traditional schools with modern ones.

Sarekat Islam (Islamic Association), the first Islamic nationalist organization in the Indies, was originally founded in 1911 as an Islamic Trading Association designed to protect Muslim merchants against ethnic Chinese competition. In 1912 the association downplayed this commercial agenda in favour of becoming a mass organization that used 'Islamic' as an equivalent of 'indigenous'. Its leader, the charismatic orator Haji Umar Said Cokroaminoto, drew thousands of listeners to his rallies. Inside of a few years, tens of thousands of supporters purchased membership cards (some believing they were amulets that would confer invulnerability), and local branches multiplied in Java and Sumatra.

Problems of organization buffeted the Sarekat Islam. After the initial enthusiasm, members stopped paying dues, and money became scarce. The Dutch agreed to recognize the organization, but only its local branches, not the central leadership. This made organizational discipline and a consistent policy impossible. Cokroaminoto favoured cooperation with the Indies Social Democratic Association and its successor, the Communist Party of the Indies, but others opposed him. They voted to make it impossible to be a member of both associations in 1921.

As the membership of Sarekat Islam evaporated, other Muslim organizations arose. Currents in world Islam were echoed in the

Indies. The Muhammadiyah, a modernist Islamic association promoting schools and social services, and the more conservative Nahdlatul Ulama, based in Java, both avoided open political activity, which enabled them to maintain large followings.

## SECULAR NATIONALISM

Burmese nationalists founded an umbrella organization in 1921, the General Council of Burmese Associations, in order to broaden their base of support beyond the ethnic Burman and Buddhist groups of Burma's diverse population. In the 1930s, students at the University of Rangoon led the Dobama Asiayone (We Burmese Association). They insisted they be addressed as *thakin* (master), a title previously reserved for Westerners. Among these leaders of the Thakins was U Aung San, who would try to lead Burma down a (largely) secular path rather than an exclusively Burman or Buddhist one. Even so, their motto was: 'Burma is our country; Burmese literature is our literature; Burmese language is our language.'

Indonesian secular nationalists had taken a similar motto in 1928, 'one land, one people, one language: Indonesia'. With that, Malay became the Indonesian language and the Netherlands Indies had a new name. These nationalists were mostly Muslims, but they did not favour an exclusively Muslim party; many of them admired Marxism. They were responsible for founding the Perserikatan Nasional Indonesia or PNI (Indonesian Nationalist Association) in 1927. Its leader would be Sukarno, a gifted orator who had once been close to Cokroaminoto of the Sarekat Islam and would become the first president of independent Indonesia. In the Netherlands, Indonesian students also infused the local student association with nationalist ideas. Secular nationalists who studied there included the later vice-president Mohammed Hatta and a prime minister of independent Indonesia, Sutan Syahrir.

Nationalist groups, all of them small and drawn from the tiny educated elite, proliferated in the Indies. They split further in the 1930s into two groups, the 'cooperating', who participated in the small and largely non-representative political councils set up by the colonial government at national and city levels (in particular the Volksraad or people's council), and the 'non-cooperating', who boycotted these institutions. The Dutch repressed non-cooperating nationalists, arresting and finally exiling leaders like Sukarno, Hatta and Syahrir. At the end of the 1930s, Indonesian nationalism in all its varieties was divided, weak and deprived of leadership.

U Aung San, leader of the Burmese nationalist Thakin movement. He was about to become the Republic of Burma's first prime minister when, on the eve of independence, he and several members of his intended cabinet were massacred by gunmen allied to a political opponent.

A corps of servants in Java attend to the wishes of their Dutch masters at dinner on a veranda. This photograph aptly illustrates the Western colonial domination that ended with the Japanese occupation and subsequent independence.

Except for the Philippines, where the Americans had begun the transition to independence in prewar years, and possibly Burma, where local people took responsibility for certain ministries in the colonial administration, independence for Southeast Asian colonies seemed a remote prospect in 1940. Then, in that year, the Japanese occupied French Indochina, at first leaving the French authorities at their posts. In December 1941, with the attack on Pearl Harbor, they marched through Siam into Burma and Malaya and Singapore. Indonesians welcomed the arrival of these Asian conquerors. In March 1942, the Dutch East Indies formally surrendered to the invaders, and by May, with the fall of the last of the American fortresses in the Philippines, all of Southeast Asia was in Japanese hands.

## CHAPTER SIX

# Violence and Transition
## *Occupation, Independence and Cold War*

The few years of Japanese occupation up to 1945 changed Southeast Asia's landscape, bringing new social currents to the fore and the end of colonialism within reach. Nationalists gained new self-assurance as they watched their former colonial overlords face military and personal humiliation at the hands of the Japanese. However, they were to inherit violence, division, shortages and disorder, which troubled their nations sometimes for decades.

Most new nations entered a period of limited democratic government. 'Charismatic' leaders sometimes overrode democratic forms. Corruption, known before, became an ingrained problem, and excessive dependence on raw material exports was a serious disadvantage when prices fell in the 1950s. Many states experienced the politicization of the military, sometimes ending in military or other authoritarian rule. The Cold War overshadowed international relations and brought prolonged war in Indochina.

### JAPANESE OCCUPATION
During the 1930s, Japanese investments in small business and trade, plantation agriculture and lumbering penetrated the region, and its political influence was growing. As Japan became more powerful, many Southeast Asian nationalists hoped it would support their cause. Tokyo recruited and trained young leaders and invited many to visit Japan.

By 1940, Japanese forces had advanced through China to the northern border of Indochina. German victory over France soon offered Japan a chance to gain control of French Indochina. The

Vichy government, ruling in southern France and the colonies (the north of France was occupied by Germany), agreed to permit Japan to use Indochina for military purposes. French colonial officials, from governor down to policeman, remained at their posts.

America, Britain and the government of the Netherlands Indies (the Netherlands itself had been under German occupation since May 1940) recognized the strategic advantage this gave Japan and responded with trade embargoes. The Japanese finally launched a pre-emptive attack against American forces with the goal of controlling the resources of all Southeast Asia. The air strike on Pearl Harbor, Hawaii, in December 1941 led to war with Britain, America and the Netherlands Indies.

From Indochina, Japan moved swiftly south- and westward. Almost immediately, it sent an ultimatum to Thailand (as Siam had been called since 1939), backed up by land and air attacks, demanding that it declare war on the Allies and permit transit of Japanese armies. The Allies could not meet Thailand's requests for help, and its military government, not unsympathetic to Japan, saw no alternative to cooperation. The Japanese promised to respect Thailand's independence. They helped it regain border territories lost to Britain and France, and spared it some of the tragic disruption experienced elsewhere in Southeast Asia. Nonetheless, many prominent Thai opposed this policy of cooperation. The Thai ambassador in Washington never delivered the declaration of war with the US, leaving open a useful loophole for the time after Japan's defeat. Others formed a 'Free Thai' movement in the jungle, which by 1944 had infiltrated the Bangkok government.

Little could stop, or even delay, Japan's thrust in 1942. Japanese troops invaded Burma, bringing with them the Thirty Comrades, young Burmans given military training by Japan. Among these were Aung San and Ne Win; their Burma Independence Army fought alongside the

The sultan of one of Borneo's petty states greets a Japanese officer in 1942. Although the Malay and Bornean aristocracy were sometimes accused of collaboration with the Japanese, in fact there was friction, and sometimes worse: in Indonesian West Borneo (Kalimantan), the Japanese massacred the local sultans and other leaders.

Japanese against the British, although Japanese troops bore the brunt of the struggle.

Other invaders moved south through Malaya, often on bicycles, and often welcomed by local people. British forces were unprepared, and many had been diverted to the European front. Isolating Singapore from the mainland, the Japanese punished the city with air attacks, forcing it to surrender. The British naval base there was a pivot of Allied defence in the region and was heavily fortified against attack by sea; in the event, it fell to attack by land. The Netherlands Indies surrendered on 8 March 1942, after landings backed by air power. Before they invaded Java, the Japanese spread leaflets printed with a prophecy attributed to the Javanese prophet Joyoboyo. This forecast that the island would be governed for three hundred years by white men, who would then be driven away by yellow men, who would themselves remain for an 'age of maize'. Then Java would become free. 'Remember Joyoboyo,' they said. Maize ripens in just ninety days, but the Japanese were to stay for over three years.

A second movement took Japanese forces into the Philippines and toward the island of Borneo. In May 1942 the last bases in the Philippines fell, though some Philippine units were soon organizing resistance.

East and Southeast Asia's occupied territories were to form what the Japanese called a 'Greater East Asian Co-Prosperity Sphere' – in other words, they would supply raw materials and labour for Japan's war machine. The occupiers also enforced economic autarky or self-sufficiency, and sometimes required that industrial crops such as jute be planted on rice lands, causing grave food shortages. Allied submarines ended the fantasy of 'co-prosperity' in late 1943, when they gained control of the long-distance shipping lanes to Japan, making transport of materials from or to Southeast Asia impossible.

As occupying rulers the Japanese were both popular and repellent. Japan assured its new subjects that Asians were vastly superior to white men and were beneficiaries of a new Asian solidarity. Many Southeast Asians moved, during the war, into positions and responsibilities previously reserved to Westerners. In other respects, the new overlords were more disturbing: Japanese often seemed arrogant or insulting to Southeast Asians, and those who opposed them were imprisoned, tortured or killed. Japan was ruling Southeast Asia even more oppressively than had the previous colonizers.

Japanese soldiers lower the American flag over Corregidor in the Philippines, after the base finally surrendered to the invaders in 1942. The event marked the achievement of Japanese rule over all of Southeast Asia.

## MOBILIZATION

Mass organizations were established with the aim of generating support for Japan's wartime goals. The occupiers also encouraged some political mobilization, a break with the colonial emphasis on peace, order and the depoliticization of subject populations.

Young men were forcibly recruited to labour battalions. Although the Allies still remember the fate of Western prisoners of war who built the 'railway of death' between Burma and Thailand, the toll among these anonymous *romusha* was far greater. Of some 300,000 recruited from the Indies, perhaps half that number ever returned.

In the Indies, the Japanese quickly brought Sukarno from his place of exile in Sumatra to Jakarta (as Batavia was now called). They gave him, Mohammed Hatta, and other prewar opposition leaders the task of supporting the war effort through anti-Allied propaganda and by encouraging mobilization of labour and supplies. Sukarno, an admirer of Japan in prewar days, nonetheless also attempted to promote the idea of Indonesian independence over the Japanese-controlled radio (sets not tuned to official frequencies were strictly forbidden). A variety of organizations grew up, including those for women, boys and young men. The Japanese initially favoured Islamic leaders, but then withdrew from this strategy, perhaps because of an incident (among others) in which a prominent religious teacher refused publicly to perform the obligatory bow toward Tokyo to the emperor. Muslims do not bow to mere emperors.

Burmese guerillas, many of them drawn from non-Burman minority groups, harassed the Japanese occupiers and hindered their activities. The British maintained contacts with these units from India and utilized them in their invasion of Burma in 1945.

Apart from Europeans, whom they used in Indochina and, temporarily, in the Indies, the Japanese turned to the native bureaucratic elite to maintain their authority. Young nationalists who had supported the Japanese invasion found themselves shunted aside. This may have encouraged the Burmese nationalist Aung San to break with the Japanese and offer his support to the British before their invasion of Burma in 1945. In the Indies, the population in some regions was so alienated by the cooperation of local elites in the mobilization of manpower and the requisitioning of essential goods that these elites became targets of bloody reprisals during the Indonesian Revolution.

## JAPANESE-TRAINED ARMIES

Young men, out of work and school (for many schools had closed), eagerly joined military and paramilitary units founded by the Japanese, sometimes in hopes of getting regular meals. Discipline was harsh, drill exacting and physical training demanding. Political indoctrination was anti-Western and anti-democratic. Many were caught up in the spirit of loyalty, comradeship and self-sacrifice.

The oldest such unit was the Burma Independence Army, which had accompanied the Japanese invasion. It continued to recruit young men, changing its name to the Burma National Army, but lost its enthusiasm for working with the Japanese. When Aung San went over to the British, the BNA helped them capture Rangoon, after having exacted a promise of independence. After 1948, the army of independent Burma absorbed the BNA as well as units that had cooperated with the British during the entire war, most of them recruited from non-Burman minorities.

Although the Japanese did not control Vietnam directly until March 1945, they began recruiting paramilitary groups even before then, including some from the sects Hoa Hao and Cao Dai (see p. 86). Paramilitary forces were usually not armed, but they were in a position to seize arms when Japan surrendered six months later.

In 1944, the Japanese formed Peta (Pembela Tanah Air, Defenders of the Fatherland) on Java and similar organizations elsewhere. Peta was no Indonesian national army; it was organized by district, and units had little contact with one another. Peta had few weapons, but it did have Indonesian officers up to the rank of major. The Japanese distrusted these groups (one battalion of Peta rebelled in 1944) and kept them divided, as well as promoting competing Islamic militias, the Hizbullah and Sabilillah. When the Indonesian Revolution broke out, Peta formed the core of the Indonesian national army, but it faced a stubborn problem of integrating other military groups.

Japan had planned to use these various military and paramilitary units to defend the occupied territories against Allied invasion. This became less likely as war progressed, and the main Allied thrust was directed not against Southeast Asia (except for the Philippines) but against the Japanese homeland itself.

## RESISTANCE

Not all Southeast Asians welcomed Japan. Its promises of independence certainly rang hollow in the Philippines, where independence was already within reach. Although many of the

Manila elite cooperated with the Japanese, armed resistance groups formed widely, partly with American support. The gap between the collaborating elite of the cities and the resistance in the countryside, exposed to vicious reprisals, divided the nation. The Philippines became a battleground in late 1944, when the Allies began the reconquest of the islands from the Japanese. Manila was devastated as advancing units removed the Japanese house by house.

In northern Thailand, Free Thai activities attracted Allied attention. In Burma, resistance was largely reserved to minority upland ethnic groups, with whom the British maintained communication from India. In Malaya, too, resistance was largely a minority matter; there, ethnic Chinese rather than hill tribes formed its core. Malays, living predominantly in villages in the traditional economy, felt less of the war's disruption. Chinese, by contrast, caught in Malaya's urban areas or on plantations and mines, lacked even basic necessities. Politically conscious Chinese had been active since the 1930s in campaigns against Japanese aggression in China. The Japanese retaliated brutally against the Chinese community leadership, killing many outright. Repression and need drove young men to the jungle, from where the Chinese-dominated Malayan Communist Party organized resistance, forming a Malayan Peoples' Anti-Japanese Army. The British funnelled some supplies and a few agents to this and other resistance groups in the jungle. Many weapons were stockpiled and were to reappear after 1948 during the Malayan Emergency (see p. 159).

In the disorder of the 1940s, one group seized the initiative in Indochina, the Vietnam Independence League or Viet Minh. Under

Ho Chi Minh *(second from left)*, Vo Nguyen Giap and Pham Van Dong, leaders of the Viet Minh, plan their resistance to the restoration of French colonial rule.

the leadership of Ho Chi Minh's Indochinese Communist Party, now called the Vietnam Lao Dong (workers') Party, the Viet Minh united anti-colonial and anti-Japanese forces, especially in the north, near the Chinese border. It easily recruited followers in the social disarray that accompanied the terrible famine of 1944 in Tonkin.

## ECONOMIC AND SOCIAL DISRUPTION

The population in areas dependent on trade, isolated by the Japanese policy of autarky and economic control, could survive only by illegal transactions. Small traders, on foot, smuggled scarce commodities, while wooden vessels transported bulk goods across the seas, evading Allied submarines and Japanese controls. Rampant inflation, fuelled by the occupiers' resort to printing huge amounts of currency to pay for requisitions, fed black markets. In Java, the poor wore jute sacks or strips of crude rubber as sarongs. In Vietnam, the shortage of textiles left people clothed in little more than straw mats during the exceptionally cold winter of 1944–45.

The occupiers fed themselves and stockpiled goods. While some collaborators, businessmen and dealers in contraband prospered, for many Southeast Asians the war was a time of more or less intense deprivation. Diseases multiplied and children suffered from mal-nutrition and stunted growth. Allied civilians and prisoners of war, living in camps, faced sickness and starvation.

After the battle of Nanjing in China in 1937, when Japanese soldiers had rampaged and raped, the military determined to arrange for orderly sexual services. Thousands of 'comfort women' were pressed into service; only recently have they broken their silence about the abuse and humiliation they endured.

## THE END OF JAPANESE OCCUPATION

### Indonesian Independence

Dai Nippon does things differently. Everything goes quickly. They have been here only two years, and we've already been given our future independence.

These words, from a satirical short story by the Indonesian author Idrus, are spoken by the head of a women's organization, who is encouraging members to contribute to a Japanese celebration even though they have nothing to give.

During the occupation, the prospect of independence suddenly seemed far closer than it had in prewar years. The Japanese were willing to make promises of independence in order to buy the support of their new subjects. The reality was rather different: in 1943, they granted the Philippines and Burma nominal independence, but they retained the last word in all matters. In the Indies, by contrast, with its essential raw materials, Japan was reluctant even to hint at independence. Finally, in September 1944, Tokyo promised independence 'in the future' (perhaps provoking Idrus' satire). In early 1945, an Investigating Committee for the Preparation of Indonesian Independence was organized in Java, led by Sukarno and including a wide spectrum of politicians, although no Communists.

In early August 1945, with Japanese defeat an immediate prospect, Sukarno and Hatta were summoned to the Japanese headquarters in Saigon to be told that Japan had finally agreed to independence. Two days after the Japanese surrender, the Indonesian nationalist leaders produced this sober declaration:

We the people of Indonesia hereby declare INDONESIAN INDEPENDENCE. Matters concerning the transfer of power and so forth will be carried out in an appropriate manner and in as short a time as possible.

Jakarta, 17 August 1945
In the name of the Indonesian people
Sukarno-Hatta

*Vietnam*

In March 1945, the Japanese incarcerated French officials and instituted ersatz independence in Indochina under the traditional monarchs, Emperor Bao Dai in Hue (Annam), King Norodom Sihanouk of Cambodia, and King Sisavang Vong of Luang Prabang-Laos. Bao Dai called himself Emperor of Vietnam, and certainly claimed authority over all three Vietnamese regions, but in reality Tonkin was already in a near-ungovernable state due to famine, banditry and Viet Minh activities, and it was impossible to know whether his authority extended to Cochin China.

On 19 August, the Viet Minh converged on Hanoi to welcoming crowds. On 2 September 1945, before a mass rally, Ho Chi Minh proclaimed the Democratic Republic of Vietnam (DRV), declaring that 'Vietnam has the right to enjoy freedom and independence….' Bao Dai was coaxed into abdicating and recognizing the new state, which quickly established authority in the north. In the south, a plethora of groups, sects, Trotskyists, criminal associations, nationalists and monarchists competed, often violently, with the Viet Minh.

Under the terms of surrender, Japan was responsible for keeping order everywhere until the colonial powers could return. The US had already occupied the Philippines and the British had expelled the Japanese from Burma, but the Japanese controlled British Malaya, French Indochina and the Netherlands Indies. The British had enough troops to occupy Malaya, but not before unprecedented race riots broke out between Malays and Chinese settling scores over collaboration.

The British were to occupy most of Indonesia until the Dutch could bring in reinforcements. Indochina below the 16th parallel was also assigned to the British. North of this line it was up to forces from Nationalist China to maintain order until the French could reassume authority. Chinese troops plundered northern Vietnam, but they also permitted the Viet Minh to secure their political foothold. The British aided the restoration of French rule in southern Indochina; the situation in Indonesia soon escaped their control.

## THE INDOCHINA WARS

The Indochina Wars still overshadow most other events in postwar Southeast Asia. They led to a massive and intrusive American presence not just in Indochina but in the entire region, just as it was trying to divest itself of colonial rule. The declaration of the Democratic Republic of Vietnam in September 1945 did not result in the establishment of Viet Minh control over the country. Instead, the French immediately moved with British help to restore authority below the 16th parallel. Only after months of negotiations between the French, Nationalist China and the Viet Minh could French officials return to the area north of that parallel, in February 1946. The Viet Minh also negotiated with the French about a transition to independence, but no real basis for Viet Minh–French cooperation existed. Postwar France itself was politically too divided, and too convinced of the importance of the colonies, to reach agreement.

In the Mekong Delta in 1950 a French soldier brings in Viet Minh prisoners. The French were able to control urban areas and major lines of communication, but in the countryside, especially in the north, entire areas were ruled by the Viet Minh.

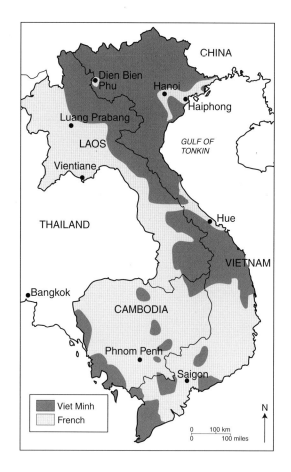

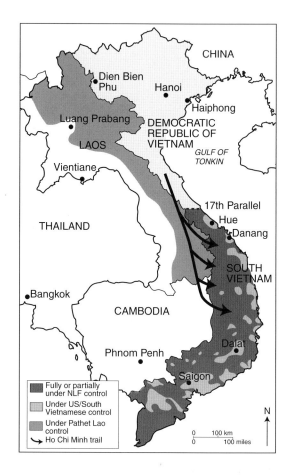

*(Above)* Indochina in April 1954, showing the approximate extent of French and Viet Minh control.

*(Above right)* Indochina by May 1965. US–South Vietnamese forces controlled a collection of discrete areas in South Vietnam; the remainder was fully or partially in the hands of the National Liberation Front, supported by the DRV and the Pathet Lao.

After months of tension, French forces finally bombarded the harbour of Hanoi, Haiphong, in December 1946, launching what has come to be called the First Indochina War. The Viet Minh withdrew from Hanoi, but managed to retain control of a 'liberated area' of perhaps a million inhabitants, cooperating especially with hill peoples in the mountains. There, revolutionary policies could be implemented. Elsewhere the Viet Minh built up structures of government in parallel to Bao Dai's ineffective regime, which the French had restored. Although French troops soon occupied all major cities of Vietnam, the Viet Minh maintained its strength in the countryside and in the north. In the south, the Bao Dai government had no genuine independence from the French. In addition, much of its territory was divided among sects such as Hoa Hao and Cao Dai, with their own military forces, and criminal and warlord elements, as well as Viet Minh-controlled zones.

The colonial war, which absorbed half a million troops, was going badly for France. The decision to withdraw was facilitated when the Viet Minh overran a major French emplacement at Dien Bien Phu, and the warring parties finally reached an accord in 1954 at an international conference in Geneva. The opposing armies would regroup, the Viet Minh–DRV north of the 17th parallel, the French, together with the 'State of Vietnam' under Bao Dai, to the south. At the demarcation line would be a Demilitarized Zone. After two years, general elections in Vietnam would decide the fate of the whole country. Other Geneva agreements called for the withdrawal of pro-Communist units from all of Cambodia and part of Laos.

With the intensification of the Cold War, the Communist victory in China in 1949, and the outbreak of the Korean War in 1950, Washington increasingly viewed the fate of Indochina as central to the 'containment' of an expansionist China and USSR. A Viet Minh–DRV victory would threaten US security by endangering the neutrality of Cambodia and Laos and, it was feared, open all of Southeast Asia to a Communist thrust in which states would fall like a row of dominoes. Consequently America was soon supporting the French with large amounts of weapons, though not yet with

*(Below left)* A street vendor takes quick advantage of the French withdrawal from the north of Vietnam after 1954: his wares include Communist flags and badges, and pin-ups of Ho Chi Minh, the USSR's Malenkov and China's Mao Zedong.

*(Below)* Ngo Dinh Diem, president of the Republic of Vietnam (the area south of the 17th parallel), makes a public broadcast in defence of his policies. Never a truly popular figure, Diem alienated many previous supporters in the course of his rule, finally losing even the Americans.

American troops. The US was dissatisfied with the Geneva accords, and particularly with plans for nationwide elections; it well knew that in a popular vote, Ho Chi Minh would win.

The Americans decided to support an ambivalent figure, Ngo Dinh Diem, a mandarin by temperament and a Catholic, but a nationalist and fervent anti-Communist, who in 1954 was Bao Dai's prime minister. Diem acted, with American advisors in the shadows, to assert full control over the State of Vietnam's territory in the south. He bought out or fought against competitors for power such as the sects and criminal bands. Viet Minh elements went into hiding or moved north. Having consolidated his power, in 1955 Diem deposed Bao Dai and declared a Republic of Vietnam in the area south of the 17th parallel, with its capital at Saigon and himself as president. In that same year (with American backing), he refused to participate in discussions with the DRV about elections, thus nullifying those provisions of the Geneva accords.

In the north, the DRV was greatly weakened by its all-out effort at Dien Bien Phu, while the implementation of Communist policies, especially the collectivization of agriculture, had aroused resistance in some areas. The country needed a breathing space. At first, it took no action on elections and reunification, although reunification was always a major goal.

Some Viet Minh cadres had remained in the south, and they soon were able to unite with other elements opposed to Diem. These

By the late 1960s the Communist National Liberation Front for South Vietnam (NLF) controlled some areas of south Vietnam so securely that it was able to maintain its own administration there. Here, a school teacher gives instruction to her pupils in a village in Quang Tri province.

included dissatisfied members of sects and others who became victims of Diem's repressive style of rule. In December 1960, a new National Liberation Front for South Vietnam (NLF) was finally established. Its propaganda consistently spoke of the Republic of Vietnam as My Diem – US-Diem – thus branding it a puppet of the Americans and a collaborator in foreign rule. Other cadres, some originally from the south, were also now infiltrating from the DRV to bolster resistance.

Anti-Diem incidents in the south and acts of terror against officials multiplied. The Americans were by now strongly committed to Diem, but while he accepted their aid, he refused their advice, preferring to rely primarily on fellow Catholics, especially members of his family. By 1961, insurgency was a serious challenge in the countryside.

Rejecting American recommendations for meaningful land reform, Diem instead moved rural people into over three thousand 'strategic hamlets', fortified villages that were intended to resist the rebels' attacks. Although this kind of resettlement had worked during the Malayan Emergency (see p. 159), here the hamlets alienated the uprooted population without providing security. Diem was rapidly losing control of the countryside; his government could not stem the advance of the NLF, which Diem and the Americans called the Viet Cong (Vietnamese Communists).

Opposition to Diem now surfaced in urban areas; Diem responded with violence to Buddhist protests against his regime. The Americans turned the tables and moved to support anti-Diem forces in a coup d'état on 1 November 1963 that left Diem and his brother Ngo Dinh Nhu dead. The political situation in Saigon disintegrated and there was a succession of leadership changes until General Nguyen Van Thieu assumed control in June 1965.

The US had gradually increased its involvement, sending some 16,000 military advisors and massive financial aid. Even so, by early 1965 the NLF and its allies in Hanoi perceived that they were close to winning the war in the south; Washington concurred. Faced with the imminent 'loss of Vietnam', for domestic political reasons an unacceptable outcome, President Lyndon Johnson decided in February of that year to authorize bombing north of the Demilitarized Zone at the 17th parallel and, later, in NLF-controlled areas in the south. When this failed to break the NLF, he officially committed ground troops, obtaining from Congress not a declaration of war but a resolution of approval to use armed force against

A North Vietnamese cartoonist's vision of the Vietnam quagmire. It depicts 'the fate of the US aggressors' in the north – graveyards of fallen aeroplanes – and in the south – troops literally sinking to their deaths.

Vietnam following an incident involving US and DRV ships in the Gulf of Tonkin in August. By the end of 1965, the Vietnam War was an American war; Diem had already cast aside French advisors in the 1950s, and now even South Vietnam's military was shunted aside as American troops and weapons poured in.

The US had pulled itself into a colonial war similar to, but more violent than, that waged by France. Its opponents, with less money and fewer arms, for the most part maintained control of both the terrain and the initiative. Attempts to clear areas of guerillas by aerial bombardment drove hundreds of thousands of refugees into the cities, while deliberate defoliation ruined large swaths of forest. Mounting American casualties fuelled anti-war sentiment in the US. Although it attempted to take the war north by bombarding DRV targets, the US was always constrained by the fear of drawing in China or the Soviet Union, both of which increasingly supported the DRV with weapons and advisors.

In February 1968, at the time of Tet, the Vietnamese New Year festivities, the NLF forces managed to occupy the old royal capital of Hue for nearly a month and even temporarily invaded the US embassy compound in Saigon. Militarily, the net effect of the Tet offensive was a devastating loss for the NLF (perhaps 40,000 casualties). But by invading and occupying urban areas, the NLF showed Americans at home that the war was not going as their leaders claimed and that victory was probably unattainable. Popular reaction led the US government to reduce the bombing and begin peace negotiations with representatives of the DRV, the NLF and the Republic of Vietnam in Paris in May 1968.

Lyndon Johnson announced after Tet that he would not run for a second term as US president. His successor, Richard Nixon, took office in January 1969, but the change of leadership had no effect on the progress of peace talks, which, like the fighting, dragged on. After Tet the NLF depended increasingly on men and supplies from

Hundreds of Vietnamese families fled the fighting in Hue at the time of the Tet Offensive of 1968, when NLF forces seized the city and held it for a month before being expelled again by American and South Vietnamese troops.

American Iriquois helicopters airlift infantrymen on a 'search and destroy' mission in the South Vietnamese countryside. The introduction of this modern equipment still could not turn the tide in the Second Indochina War.

the north. Its lifeline was a network of roads and paths through Laos that was popularly dubbed the Ho Chi Minh Trail. The NLF also maintained bases in supposedly neutral Cambodia, although it denied this at the time. The DRV became dependent on aid from the Soviet Union, the only source of modern weapons to repulse high-tech American attacks, especially those from the air.

Nixon's war policy entailed the 'Vietnamization' of the war: withdrawing American ground troops and instead supplying an augmented Army of the Republic of Vietnam with ample war material. Peace talks, but also bombing, continued. In the spring of 1972, the NLF, now taking orders from the 120,000-strong DRV army, undertook a major surprise offensive. Although initially successful, these forces met massive American air power in both the north and the south and suffered very high casualties, perhaps double those incurred in the Tet offensive. Nixon also ordered the bombing of the harbour of Hanoi, off-limits to his predecessors because of the fear that Soviet or Chinese ships might be inadvertently hit. His active foreign policy of détente with the Soviet Union and his approach to the People's Republic of China had partially neutralized these partners of the DRV.

That same year a peace agreement was finally drafted by negotiators Henry Kissinger and Le Duc Tho. This provided for American withdrawal and rule by a coalition drawn from the Saigon government of President Thieu, some southern neutralists and the

NLF. When Thieu refused to accept the terms of the agreement, however, and talks broke down, Nixon ordered renewed bombing of North Vietnam in December, even though the DRV was not the source of the problem. Finally, Hanoi signalled its acquiescence and a treaty was signed on 27 January 1973. Thieu was persuaded to sign by an American promise to resort to force should the DRV break the treaty. America's longest war had ended; it cost 59,000 American dead and millions of killed, wounded and displaced Vietnamese.

The Americans' threatened resort to force never happened. They had effectively removed their ground forces from Vietnam, and although huge supplies of weapons were shipped to the south, which might have enabled it to withstand a DRV onslaught, the US never again intervened. When in January 1975 the DRV launched a major offensive against the south, Richard Nixon was no longer in office, the US Congress had passed legislation against further American military involvement in Indochina, and southern resistance quickly collapsed. On 30 April 1975, Saigon fell to the Communists. Newspapers around the world published photographs of the last American officials scrambling to their helicopters, leaving desperate Vietnamese collaborators to their fate.

Saigon was renamed Ho Chi Minh City, and remaining southern leaders – Thieu had already left the country – were arrested. Talk of a coalition was forgotten as the NLF and North Vietnamese quickly took control. Despite promises that reunification would be a gradual process, by May 1976 it was already a *fait accompli*. North and South now formed the Socialist Republic of Vietnam.

## CAMBODIA AND LAOS

War in Vietnam inevitably spilled over into other parts of Indochina. Laos was the first country to be caught up in hostilities, partly because the Viet Minh were trying to win the support of hill peoples on both sides of the long border. Laos' fragile unity was already threatened in 1954, when the pro-Viet Minh Pathet Lao were in control of much of the north. The Geneva Accords of 1954 brought a partial withdrawal, but Pathet Lao forces were soon entrenched again.

By 1962, Laos was a battleground between pro- and anti-Communist forces, the latter clandestinely supported by the USA. In that year, the Soviet Russians and the US decided to reach a peace settlement to prevent Laos from generating a wider international conflict. In effect, the country was partitioned. As the war in Vietnam

*(Left)* Protests in Phnom Penh against intense US bombing of Cambodian terrain. Years later, the North Vietnamese finally admitted they had constructed bases within Cambodian territory, though they – and Sihanouk *(below)* – vigorously denied it at the time.

*(Above)* A Buddhist monk teaches well-armed pupils in a Pathet Lao-controlled village in Laos. The Neo Lao Haksat, the political wing of the Pathet Lao, attempted to manage a literacy campaign at the same time as fighting a war.

*(Right)* Many Filipinos fought alongside American troops in a guerilla war against the Japanese, and in early 1945 the question of collaboration with the enemy, especially by members of the elite, became a divisive one. Here the American leader of an anti-Japanese unit accuses a Chinese–Filipino of spying for Japan.

148

grew in intensity, Laos was drawn into the conflict again by the Ho Chi Minh Trail, the paths running through the country that supplied insurgents in southern Vietnam. The Americans continued to intervene, choosing the Hmong tribesmen as their stand-ins against pro-DRV forces, and bombing targets where they presumed the trail to be. In 1971, South Vietnamese forces invaded Laos, looking for Communist sanctuaries. Their quick defeat helped show the Americans that the Vietnamization of the war (see p. 146) was no solution.

In 1975, Laos fell entirely to Pathet Lao forces under Kaysone Phomvihane, who became prime minister. The monarchy gave way, under duress, to the Lao People's Democratic Republic.

Cambodia was also a battleground in 1954, when the Geneva accords sealed its independence. Although King Norodam Sihanouk (after 1955, when he abdicated, he was called Prince) insisted that pro-Viet Minh forces had evacuated Cambodian territory, as stipulated in the Geneva agreements, in fact many remained or soon returned. In March 1970, Sihanouk was removed from office by the incompetent General Lon Nol, who was pro-American. The deposed leader fled to exile in Beijing. Already in 1969, the US had begun secret bombing of regions where Communist bases were suspected – a clear violation of Cambodia's neutrality. In May of that year, American and South Vietnamese forces invaded neighbouring Cambodian territory in defiance of Cambodian sovereignty and neutrality. The invasion caused renewed anti-war protests in the US; an act of Congress forced Nixon to withdraw ground forces. In 1973, however, Nixon initiated heavy bombing of Cambodian territory. The devastation of these attacks drove people into the hands of a rebel group that Sihanouk had already dubbed the Khmer Rouge (Red Khmer).

Social disorder increased. Lon Nol's army was inept, with corrupt officers and unpaid men. Khmer Rouge control increased, and in April 1975 they marched into a Phnom Penh bloated by war refugees and urban profiteers. Only later did international observers realize that these men were by no means allies of the DRV.

## INDEPENDENCE IN OTHER COUNTRIES

### Philippines

Washington felt that the wartime division and devastation of the Philippines should not delay the planned transition to independence. On 4 July 1946, American Independence Day, the transfer of power

took place in Manila. Unsolved problems now lay in the lap of the new Republic of the Philippines.

Among them was the question of elite collaboration with the Japanese. US General Douglas MacArthur, who had served in the colony before the war, settled the problem at one stroke by insisting that his personal friend, Manuel Roxas, was innocent of collaboration. With that, the idea of even censuring collaborators was off the table, Roxas could be elected president, and power returned securely to the old elite, which was closely linked to the landlord class.

In 1948, with support from the large and growing number of landless in central Luzon, a Communist-led former guerilla group, the Hukbalahap, rebelled in protest against corrupt national politics and arbitrary exercise of power by rural landlords. Only reforms under then Secretary of Defence Ramon Magsaysay enabled the rebellion to be suppressed. Magsaysay became president in 1953. An immensely popular figure, he 'understood', as David Steinberg asserts, 'as perhaps no Filipino politician has before or since, the legitimate grievances of the peasantry.' He died before

Ramon Magsaysay makes a gesture of triumph after his election to president of the Philippines in 1953. He won an overwhelming victory against his corrupt and unpopular predecessor, but was tragically killed in an aeroplane accident before the end of his term.

the end of his term in a plane crash in 1956.

The US continued to dominate the Philippine economy. Agreements giving it preferential trade conditions allowed Americans unlimited rights to do business and acquire land. Defence agreements also enabled the US to retain huge military bases with practically extraterritorial rights. These were to become a keystone of American Cold War policy in the Pacific, and especially in Indochina.

Many Filipinos resented this continuing dominance of the US in Philippine affairs. Still, it meant that the country was able to leave the responsibility – and costs – of national defence in American hands, and the Philippine military remained relatively apolitical. Philippine nationalism, in practice limited to the educated and politically active elite, grew more potent in subsequent decades.

### Burma

General Aung San had laid the grounds for Burmese independence with his cooperation with Japan and then with Britain (see p. 134), but tragedy overshadowed the transition. In July 1947, armed men broke into a pre-independence cabinet session and in a few minutes gunned down Aung San and six other leaders of the dominant

Anti-Fascist People's Freedom League, a coalition of prewar nationalist groups and representatives of the minorities. Thakin U Nu, unprepared and not a member of cabinet, would become the first prime minister.

Independence came peacefully on 4 January 1948, at an hour astrologers found propitious, but the diverse and conflicting interests in the ruling Anti-Fascist People's Freedom League eventually led to its disintegration. Communist elements soon turned to armed resistance. The Karen minority living in the Irrawaddy delta not far from the capital, many of whom were Christian, rebelled against a Burman-Buddhist-led government, as did other minorities in the

The ceremonial unveiling of a bronze statue of Aung San in February 1955 in Rangoon. Prime Minister U Nu urged all attending to rededicate themselves to the unfinished work of the deceased nationalist leader.

Nationalization of industries in Burma under the dictatorship of General Ne Win had reached even this small distillery–brewery in Mandalay by 1969. In recent years Burma has sought some foreign investment, but socialism remains the watchword.

uplands. Troops from Nationalist China, fleeing the Communist advance, crossed into northern Burma, settling beyond the control of the central government; their territory would later become a major channel of international drug traffic. By late 1948 Rangoon was nearly isolated. Only slowly, but never completely, was security restored.

In foreign relations, Burma adopted a policy of strict non-alignment, rejecting membership of the Commonwealth. At home, major industries were nationalized. The 1953 Land Nationalization Act deprived non-farming owners of their land; thus most rural land previously acquired by Indian moneylenders was restored to Burmese farmers, and many Indians left the country. Impatient with the failures of civilian politicians, the army assumed dictatorial power in 1962.

## Indonesia

The Indonesian Revolution of 1945–49 combined both military resistance and diplomatic negotiations. The involvement of the United Nations in these negotiations internationalized the struggle.

In 1945, the Japanese attitude to Indonesian independence was divided. Peta units scrambled to obtain weapons, and though some

Japanese willingly gave them, others forcibly resisted attacks on arms depots. The Republic created an Indonesian national army from former Peta units, Islamic militias, and politically-linked youth groups, all more loyal to their individual leaders than to national political leaders. Division among the military would plague the Republic for years.

British troops, landing in September to disarm the Japanese, found themselves facing a revolution. Fierce Indonesian resistance in the East Javanese port of Surabaya in November 1945 convinced them that their task was impossible unless they cooperated with the Sukarno-Hatta government. The Dutch, now leaving prisoner-of-war (or civilian concentration) camps, or filtering back from abroad, found an entirely unfamiliar situation.

The restored colonial administration wanted Indonesia's resources to rebuild the Netherlands' war-damaged economy. It quickly established authority in most of the Outer Islands, where it would have access to the raw materials gaining high prices on the world market. Despite early fighting and two 'Police Actions' in 1947 and 1948 that gave the Dutch forces control of almost all major cities (and in the second of which Sukarno and Hatta were captured), continued attacks from the countryside threatened their lines of communication.

The Republic was internally divided. In 1948, disappointed with the official policy of negotiating with the Dutch, an Islamic group in West Java broke away to establish a Darul Islam, a 'House of Islam' that fought first the Dutch and then the Republic until 1962. In September 1948, army units and sympathizers of the reconstituted Communist Party (PKI) rebelled in Central and East Java, near Madiun. The Madiun Rebellion was quickly extinguished and sympathizers killed or jailed. The military was left with a distrust of both Islamic fervour and Communist radicalism.

The changed attitude of the USA, which after Madiun dropped its tendency to support the Dutch, combined with United Nations efforts for peace, forced the Netherlands to negotiate in earnest. In December 1949 a Round Table Conference reached an agreement for the transfer of sovereignty to a new Indonesian state, with a continued role for the Netherlands crown. This federal state included a number of non-republican 'states' established under

The Dutch captured the leadership of the Indonesian Republic in December 1948, hoping to end its resistance. Here, President Sukarno and Foreign Minister Haji Agus Salim are pictured in detention on Bangka in April 1949. In fact Sukarno was released just a few months later, as guerilla warfare and international diplomacy drove the Dutch to the bargaining table.

Sovereignty was formally transferred from the Netherlands to Indonesia on 27 December 1949. At the ceremony in The Hague, Mohammed Hatta (centre, with glasses) led the Indonesian delegation, while Queen Juliana and Prime Minister M. Drees (right) represented the Netherlands.

The status of West New Guinea (West Irian to Indonesians) remained unresolved in 1949. The grafitti read 'the Dutch must go', 'take West Irian' and 'throw out the Dutch'. In 1962, the Netherlands agreed to cede West Irian to Indonesia, although an independence movement there has resisted Indonesian rule.

Dutch protection during 1946–48, whose representatives in the federal parliament outnumbered those of the Republic. It was agreed that the Dutch should retain West New Guinea – called West Irian by Indonesians – until further negotiations, although it was clearly part of the old Netherlands Indies.

The rickety federal structure gave way to a unitary republic in August 1950. By 1956, it was clear that the Netherlands had no intention of negotiating the return of West New Guinea. In the following year Indonesia confiscated all Dutch assets in the Republic, provoking an exodus of Netherlands citizens, many of them Eurasians.

Political divisions plagued the young republic. Since the great majority of Indonesians profess Islam, the role of Islam in politics seemed assured, but how to define it? Secular nationalists opposed an 'Islamic state'. Sukarno, in a still-remembered speech of July 1945, offered an all-encompassing ideology that subsumed all religions in the Pancasila or five principles. These were: nationalism, democracy, socialism, humanitarianism, and belief in God. Pancasila was enshrined in the Indonesian Constitution of 1945, but the issue of Islam's role was only postponed.

Other divisions stemmed from Indonesia's extraordinary physical and ethnic diversity. In the 1950s, cabinets were unstable multi-party coalitions, divided over foreign and domestic policy. Many hoped that the first general elections in 1955 would bring a resolution of party divisions. Instead, electoral rules and proportional representation allowed parties to proliferate. Only four parties emerged from the elections with more than five per cent of the vote. Two were Islamic: the Nahdlatul Ulama (NU, Association of Islamic Scholars) and the Masyumi (Council of Indonesian Muslim Associations). The other two were 'secular': the PNI (Nationalist Party of Indonesia, once Sukarno's movement) and the Communist PKI. The strong comeback of the Communists (with over sixteen per cent of the total vote) after the defeat of 1948 surprised many observers, and the near-equality of parliamentary votes between the Islamic and secular parties prevented any conclusive resolution of the question of whether or not Indonesia should be an Islamic state.

The 1955 election also revealed a cleft between the parties of Java and those of the Outer Islands. PNI, PKI and NU drew most of their votes from Java, especially East and Central Java. Masyumi was mostly a party of the more deeply Islamic Outer Islands and West Java. The economic interests of densely populated Java, dependent on rice imports, and those of the Outer Islands, which exported raw materials, diverged. What was perceived as a consistently pro-Java economic policy, and the later elimination of Masyumi from the cabinet, increased regional tension.

Export earnings were declining, capital plant was deteriorating, and the economy slipped into chronic inflation. Local army officers, dependent on what one

Leaders of Indonesia's two largest Muslim parties, K.H. Dahlan (left) of the Nahdlatul Ulama and former prime minister M. Natsir of the Masyumi, discuss a cabinet crisis in 1957. Natsir was later accused of supporting a regional rebellion, incarcerated without trial and the Masyumi abolished.

scholar called 'extra-budgetary financing', diverted export income to their own uses. As the situation worsened, the PKI increased its popularity, especially in the Javanese countryside, where it established a number of mass organizations and unsettled the army's leadership. Some outer regions rebelled against the central government, and the USA became temporarily involved by encouraging them in the late 1950s.

President Sukarno perceived the crisis as a failure of revolutionary verve. Abandoning the role of figurehead, he propounded a government of all forces, nationalist, religious and Communist (until 1959, the Communists had never been in the cabinet). He restructured parliament and banned the Masyumi on the grounds of its supposed role in regional rebellions.

From 1958 to 1965, power in Indonesia was exercised by Sukarno, the largely anti-Communist (but disunited) military, and the PKI. At the fulcrum of this unstable triangle, the president leaned increasingly toward the PKI. Under UN and US pressure, the Dutch agreed in 1962 to submit West New Guinea to a process of transition under UN and Indonesian authority. Meanwhile, Indonesia's traditionally non-aligned foreign policy tilted toward the People's Republic of China, North Vietnam and North Korea, while it waged a low-level war against Malaysia, withdrew from the United Nations, and nearly broke off relations with the USA. Economic decline continued and the rise of the PKI appeared irresistible, with party leaders in 1964 speaking of arming the workers and peasants, a challenge to the military's monopoly of force.

In the night of 30 September 1965, several army generals were kidnapped and killed. The following day, a 'Thirtieth of September Movement', headed by Lieutenant Colonel Untung of Sukarno's palace guard, proclaimed that it had prevented a planned coup by these men against the government and installed a Revolutionary Council of military and political figures. General Suharto, Commander of the Strategic Reserve, staged a counter-coup, putting the blame for the incidents on the PKI. The party proved ineffective in organizing its defence, and the military went on to isolate, arrest and kill PKI leaders in a purge that extended to the countryside and resulted in mass executions of party members and sympathizers, perhaps 500,000 persons in all. Meanwhile, students organized demonstrations against the PKI and against Sukarno, demanding he step down. On 11 March 1966, Sukarno turned over power to restore order to General Suharto, who, a year later, became acting president.

General Suharto poses with his foreign minister (and later vice-president) Adam Malik in 1967, having assumed power first as acting president and then as president. Suharto would remain in power for over three decades, until he was forced out of office in May 1998.

*Malaya and British Colonies*

The British were reluctant to move toward independence in Malaya because of the deterioration of race relations after World War II, which potentially threatened the substantial British investments in mining and plantations there. In addition Chinese and Indian immigration had left the Malays a minority in the Malayan Peninsula (including Singapore), and it was these 'immigrant races' who were best organized politically, putting them in a position to dominate the Malays. A plan was unveiled in 1946 that would have united the Peninsula, but not Singapore, into a Malayan Union. The sultans would transfer their authority to the British Crown and all citizens, including naturalized immigrants, would have equal rights. Malays, however, were suddenly politicized by this proposal and successfully campaigned against it. Subsequent proposals guaranteed rights for Malays in certain fields, especially access to agricultural land and public employment, since as *bumiputera* (sons of the soil), they had a claim, in colonial tradition, to protection. They also guaranteed the rights of the sultans. Later moves toward independence restricted access to citizenship for immigrants.

Meanwhile, in 1948, Chinese guerilla bands had withdrawn again to the jungle, from where they waged war against British installations and perpetrated terrorist attacks in an attempt to paralyse the

economy. This self-styled Malayan Races' Liberation Army claimed to unite all Malayans against colonialism and capitalism. In fact, their leadership was drawn from the Malayan Communist Party and was almost exclusively ethnic Chinese. The British, declaring a State of Emergency, pursued a policy of isolating the rebels by forcibly resettling rural Chinese and other 'squatters' who acted as their suppliers, moving them from remote areas to fortified 'New Villages' where they could be supervised. At the same time, they made political concessions toward independence to those willing to work for it peacefully. The Emergency, as it is called, died down by the early 1950s and officially ended in 1960.

In 1957, the Malayan Peninsula became independent as the Federation of Malaya. Political power was in the hands of a multi-ethnic alliance founded some years earlier by conservative Malays in the United Malays' National Organization (UMNO); the Malayan Chinese Association, which had an equally conservative, English-speaking leadership; and a party representing the Indian community, the Malayan Indian Congress. Chinese and Indians could be admitted to citizenship though birth or naturalization, but special privileges for Malays, at the time the great majority of citizens, were maintained. European and minority economic interests were guaranteed.

Singapore, still home of a major British naval base, as well as being the harbour for Malaya's export trade, remained a colony. Its predominantly Chinese population was under strong left-wing influence, and the island appeared to be becoming more and more difficult to govern. In the early 1960s, Britain sought a solution to Singapore's decolonization that would guarantee British, Malayan and other interests in the region. The British also hoped to divest themselves of their colonies in Borneo: North Borneo or Sabah (now a colony, not a private possession); Sarawak (the Brooke family had turned over their war-damaged territory to the Colonial Office); and a British protectorate, the Sultanate of Brunei.

In 1961, the Malayan prime minister who had led the country since independence, Tunku Abdul Rahman, proposed the Malaysia Plan to combine these unequal partners – Singapore, Sabah, Sarawak and Brunei – with the Federation of Malaya. Malaya's resistance to union with the Chinese-dominated city of Singapore was reduced by the inclusion of the Bornean territories, which had relatively smaller ethnic Chinese populations (about 20–25 per cent) than did the Federation of Malaya (at the time 37 per cent, with 11 per cent South Asian). Although the Tunku (as he was called) apparently

*(Opposite)* Malaya celebrates its peaceful transition to independence from the British in 1957 with a military march through Kuala Lumpur, passing in front of government buildings constructed in a unique colonial–Moorish style.

A short-lived rebellion broke out in Brunei in December 1962, with the result that the sultan scrapped plans to join the Federation of Malaysia. Here ragtag rebels make their way through the elephant grass.

thought this would ensure a majority for Malays, in reality Sarawak and Sabah had relatively few Malays. Most of their inhabitants were indigenous Bornean peoples, some of whom saw their interests as antagonistic to those of Malays. Prime Minister Lee Kuan Yew of Singapore agreed to the Plan, staging a carefully orchestrated plebiscite to win popular support for the union. However Brunei broke away from the Malaysia Plan and returned to British protection after a short-lived rebellion challenged its ruler in December 1962. It became an independent, but oil-rich, sultanate, Brunei Darussalam, in 1984.

On 16 September 1963, Malaya merged with Singapore, Sarawak and Sabah to form the Federation of Malaysia. Some powers, for example in education and control of immigration, were retained by the new member states. Indonesia immediately instituted an armed campaign against Malaysia, regarding it as a 'neo-imperialist' threat to its interests in the region, only making peace in 1966, after the fall of Sukarno. British forces effectively put down the small guerilla opposition in the Bornean jungles on behalf of Malaysia.

Conflicting economic interests and clashing political styles led Malaysia to divide. In August 1965, Singapore became independent. Lee Kuan Yew later claimed that the Malay politicians expected the city-state to 'come crawling back'. Instead, it began to court foreign investments, withstood the 1971 withdrawal of the British naval base (a major contributor to the economy), and began to grow rapidly in both production and per capita income.

### Thailand
Phibunsongkhram, a military man, ruled Siam from late 1938, when he became prime minister. He changed the name of the country to Thailand in 1939, asserting a claim to leadership of the Tai peoples

beyond Thailand's borders in neighbouring countries. Pro-Japanese, he briefly lost power in 1944 to more pro-Allied, civilian successors. Hopes for postwar civilian government failed when the young king, Ananda Mahidol (r. 1935–46), who had just returned from abroad, was found mysteriously shot, possibly murdered, in the palace in 1946. In November 1947, a 'Coup Group' of army officers, probably with Phibunsongkhram's support, seized power. In 1948 he again became prime minister, and remained in office until 1957, despite a series of attempted coups. Political freedoms were suppressed; foreign policy was pro-American and anti-Communist. When the new king, Bhumibol Adulyadej, returned to Thailand in 1951, Phibun limited his role to that of a figurehead.

Thailand struggled with authoritarian military rule from the end of the absolute monarchy in 1932 until recently. As a cohesive force, the military was well-placed in this period to exercise power over civilian politicians and bureaucrats. Fed by a constant stream of youth through compulsory service, it was (and is) led by graduates of a single military academy. The strongest image of the military in Thailand is its repeated coups and attempted coups, while the bureaucracy has played a large part in maintaining continuity.

During the early 1950s, Phibun began losing power to two associated generals, one from the police, the other, Sarit Thanarat, commander of the First Army in Bangkok. After limited democratic experiments in 1955–57, and an attempt to secure his power by holding an election, however fraudulent, Phibun yielded to Sarit in 1957. Sarit instituted a conservative and repressive dictatorship, combined with an opening to economic development. He stressed traditional Thai values, as he understood them, and maintained a close alliance with the USA. He encouraged King Bhumibol to take a public role that was without precedent for a monarch in Thailand and propagated loyalty to king, country and Buddhism.

After Sarit's death in 1963, his associates, Generals Thanom Kittikachorn (see p. 72) and Phraphas Charusathian, held on to power. By this time Communist activity in Laos and disputes with Cambodia had drawn Thailand into the troubles in Indochina. Thailand made available military bases to the US, and bombing missions against Laos and Vietnam were launched from airfields in Thailand. Bangkok catered as a rest-and-recreation area to US troops on leave. In the countryside, anti-government insurgency posed a threat, especially in the northeast, which was both culturally and geographically close to Laos.

The massacre of students in Bangkok in 1976 signalled the temporary end of a democratic experiment in Thailand. Soldiers, vigilantes and other elements forced their way into the campus and gunned down protesting students, later installing a repressive, right-wing government. Many young people fled to the jungles, returning when Thailand's politics became more open in the 1980s.

In 1973, as America was withdrawing from Vietnam, a series of student demonstrations supported by the king led to the installation of a civilian government. Elections in 1975 were the climax of a period of heady political activity, demonstrations and strikes. The democratic experiment was short-lived. The elite, witnessing the April 1975 Communist takeovers in Laos (where the monarchy was abolished) and Cambodia, became nervous, and in 1976 anti-democratic forces regrouped. When students demonstrated against the return from exile of former military dictator Thanom, right-wing vigilantes, police and others attacked. A repressive civilian government assumed control and, in 1977, a military regime took over. Many young people fled to the jungles to join Communist guerilla organizations, but most filtered back to Bangkok within a few years. In the 1980s, Thailand began a gradual return to democracy.

## CHAPTER SEVEN

# Development and Democracy
*Southeast Asia in Recent Decades*

Economic growth and liberalization and demands for political democracy are the dominant themes of Southeast Asian history over recent decades. In 1997 and 1998 serious economic and environmental crises called into question previous high rates of growth and raised questions of internal stability. Meanwhile, the regional Association of Southeast Asian Nations (ASEAN), founded in 1967, has expanded from its original five members to encompass all of Southeast Asia, though problems of integrating new members may change the nature of its previously harmonious cooperation.

ACCELERATED GROWTH

*Singapore*
Having split with Malaysia in 1965, Singapore could expect the loss of traditional sources of income and jobs, aggravated by a rapidly growing urban population. An Indonesian trade boycott in place since 1963 deprived Singapore of income from processing and re-exporting rubber and other raw materials from the Archipelago (apart from that which was smuggled in defiance of official policy). Malaysia, traditionally the port's largest customer, continued to direct most exports through Singapore, but low prices for raw materials and talk of redirecting exports to Malaysian harbours warned Singapore's leaders that new economic directions were necessary.

Today, Singaporeans like former Prime Minister (now Senior Minister) Lee Kuan Yew emphasize the disadvantages Singapore faced: traditional dependence on entrepôt activities, no hinterland, no natural resources, not even an adequate supply of drinking water.

Lee Kuan Yew, prime minister of Singapore, speaks up in the early 1960s. More recently, in his position of senior minister, the Cambridge-educated Lee has strongly pleaded for popular education in Asian, especially Confucian, values and in Chinese language.

Singapore, however, was and is one of the world's finest natural harbours, with a splendid, central location in the region. In addition, British colonialism and Chinese initiative had given Singapore a relatively well-educated population, although it was divided between an English- and a Chinese-language stream, and a relatively good infrastructure.

Politically the city was in the firm grasp of the People's Action Party, led by Lee. Left-leaning elements, especially from the Chinese-educated community, had been sidelined and many of their leaders were in jail. Nominally socialist, the PAP became in practice conservative. Its leaders were mostly English-educated and of Chinese or Indian origin, and the party had less success in attracting the Malay minority, who gravitated to the local branch of UMNO (United Malays' National Organization).

With near-total control of the legislature, the PAP opted for a technocratic approach to development. A critical problem was that of housing: much of the urban population still resided in slum conditions. Public housing, partly financed by workers' compulsory contributions to a social security plan, grew rapidly. Today 86 per cent of the population lives in these flats, many owning them outright. Strict birth-control policies reduced population growth and a number of initiatives opened up new areas of employment.

New industrial estates and favourable conditions attracted foreign investors. Once dominated by industries drawn to its low labour costs, Singapore's economy increasingly attracts industries seeking a better-qualified work force. Labour, formerly a source of serious unrest and strikes, was tamed by official policy in the 1960s. A board regulated costs to prevent wages from rising to non-competitive levels in bad years while allowing small increases in good ones. Political stability, infrastructural improvements – especially modernization of the harbour – and the upgrading of communications all contributed to a new attractiveness for investors, who came increasingly not from the former colonial power, Great Britain, but from other Western countries and Japan. Investors could also be confident of a non-corrupt bureaucracy without parallel in Southeast Asia.

PAP economic development relied on large-scale investments by international concerns and state-controlled operations like housing and communications. The city is a financial centre for the region. Another element in Singapore's economic growth has been tourism, encouraged since the 1970s by the opening of luxury hotels and shopping centres, the establishment of a national airline, and the construction of recreation sites to serve both tourists and local people. Service industries became major employers of Singaporeans.

Politics was as carefully ordered as the economy. Although the opposition is small and impotent, the government contains it by threatening to reduce social services to districts that do not support the PAP. The Chinese-language school system, considered a hotbed of radical activity in the 1950s and early 1960s, was absorbed into a national system using English as language of instruction; even the privately-founded Chinese-language university, Nanyang University, was melted into the National University of Singapore.

To some extent, Singapore, as the first 'tiger economy', became a model for economic development in the region. Its political restrictiveness and rejection of 'Western-style liberal democracy and freedoms', in the words of Prime Minister Goh Chok Tong, did not go unimitated either. By the 1980s, cracks had appeared in the facade: the low birth rate had left the island republic with an ageing population, and young families in small public housing units were reluctant to make room to care for the older generation. Emphasis on English language and modernization had left a cultural vacuum, in the eyes of the PAP at least, and the government began to re-evaluate the importance of traditional Asian cultures, especially Chinese culture. Mandarin became a required second language for those of Chinese origin, and Confucianism became the watchword of cultural revivalism, finding its way not only into schools but into the public sphere. Even the traditional Chinese associations based on family names or place of origin in China, once seen as old-fashioned and divisive, gained a new lease on life. Leaders spoke of general Asian values, but Chineseness was

Skyscrapers encroach on Chinatown in Singapore. Urban development has meant the destruction of more and more of the Asian-style shophouses once typical of the city, and has continued apace since this photograph was taken in 1983. Most Singaporeans now live in high-rise public housing.

clearly growing in importance, perhaps even surpassing Singaporean identity, once a watchword of cultural politics. Nonetheless, the island republic is surrounded and greatly outnumbered by Muslim Malays and Indonesians, and cannot insulate itself from their political and economic crises, as 1997–98 showed. After a dip in growth and prosperity, however, Singapore was soon on the path to recovery.

## AUTHORITARIAN RULE AND ECONOMIC DEVELOPMENT

The military had been entrenched in power in Thailand since the 1940s, and in the postwar decades a spate of military governments took power elsewhere in Southeast Asia. Burma's elected politicians gave way to a military regime, first temporarily, from 1958 to 1960, and then indefinitely from 1962. Indonesia's military increased its role in 1957 and took power with Suharto after 1965. Even the Philippine military became more politicized in the 1970s. On the other hand, economic development brought new middle classes and educated groups to the fore, and some made their objections felt against dictatorial and often corrupt military regimes.

### The Philippines

The Philippines fell to authoritarian government after the re-election of Ferdinand Marcos to the presidency in 1969. Faced with unrest in the capital and rebellions by Muslims and Communists in the provinces, and unable to run for a third term under the Philippine constitution, Marcos declared martial law and remained in office.

Pope John Paul II on a visit to the Philippines, Asia's only predominantly Catholic country, in 1981. Philippine president-dictator Ferdinand Marcos gives a welcoming speech, while Marcos's wife Imelda turns her attention to the pontiff. On the right, Cardinal Jaime Sin of Manila, an opponent of Marcos's dictatorial rule, watches the proceedings joylessly.

Although he claimed to be promoting economic development, in fact the Philippines underwent an economic downturn under Marcos' dictatorial regime. High prices for oil imports and low export prices for Philippine products were partly responsible for the troubles, but they were compounded by Marcos' patronage of corrupt relatives and crony capitalists, his favouritism toward new Chinese businessmen, and his attacks on established business families. The economy limped along, unable to cope with widespread poverty that was scarcely alleviated by remittances from Philippine workers abroad. The assassination of Marcos' political rival, Benigno Aquino, in August 1983, turned the tide against Marcos, whose involvement was widely suspected. Physically ailing himself, he relied more and more on the military to support his equally moribund regime.

Aquino's widow Cory became the focus of opposition to Marcos' rule. She and her supporters probably won an election held in November 1985, although ballot stuffing and other tricks enabled Marcos to claim victory. Outraged Aquino supporters, the Catholic Church, and elements of the military organized open protest, facing down tanks on Edsa (Epifanio de los Santos Avenue, a major Manila artery). Seriously ill, Marcos succumbed to American pressure to accept an offer of exile in Hawaii. 'People Power' had prevailed.

President Aquino took office on 25 February 1986. After the heady days of Edsa, her regime disappointed many. The old pre-Marcos oligarchy appeared to be returning at the expense of the poor and landless. She had to rely on the army for support (not least

The message of these youthful protesters *(below left)* is self-evident. Opposition to Marcos spread from left-wing opposition groups to other elements, including finally much of the Catholic Church and members of the elite. Corazon Cojuangco Aquino *(below)*, widow of Benigno Aquino, who was assassinated by Marcos' henchmen, became the symbol of the democratic opposition to the president and finally, after a non-violent standoff with his supporters, became president herself in 1986.

These Filipino children, playing along a railway track, represent the stubborn problems of poverty that still grip much of Philippine society. The restoration of democracy has not bettered their lot.

against attempted coups led by officers), particularly on General Fidel Ramos, who became her successor in 1992. Human rights abuses persisted, especially among the military, but there was some progress in dealing with rebellions of the Communists and of the Muslims in the south. An element of nationalist triumph accompanied the closure of American military bases in 1991. During negotiations for a new treaty that would have prolonged the increasingly resented American presence, nature and the end of the Cold War conveniently intervened. The eruption of Mount Pinatubo made Clark Air Base, once a pivot of American power in the Pacific, unusable, while the new international situation made it unnecessary. Some of the former base territory is now an industrial zone.

Ramos was a more sober leader than his predecessor, and the economy finally began to recover. In 1998 he turned over power after a single term (as the constitution now requires) and his former vice-president, Joseph Estrada, was elected to office. If 'People Power' had restored constitutional democracy, these changes of government secured it. The Philippines was less affected by the Asian financial crisis of 1997–98 than its neighbours, although growth did slow, and stubborn problems of elite control, sporadic rebel activity, poverty, population growth and environmental decay have defied solution.

### Indonesia

After the attempted coup and violence of 1965–66, President Suharto gave the military extraordinary powers in politics, security and administration. Military men assumed positions in the civilian administration from the cabinet down to village level. The 1945 Constitution, which Sukarno had reinstated in 1959, allowed for a strong presidency at the expense of parliament. Over the years, the government manipulated the opposition parties in various ways, influencing their choice of leadership, their political platforms (Islamic symbolism was not permitted; instead all parties had to express loyalty to Pancasila, see p. 155), and even the number of their votes. Only three political parties could participate in elections: the government-sponsored Golkar (Golongan Karya, or functional groups), an Islamic party and a non-Islamic one. Golkar consistently won about two-thirds of the votes in elections held between 1971 and 1997, thanks to support from the military and bureaucracy.

Legitimation of this authoritarian rule lay in the heritage and traditions of revolutionary times – the 1945 Constitution, Pancasila, and the so-called 'dual function' of the military in both defence and internal order. The most important legitimation was economic development, orchestrated by technocrats and national planners. Thanks to improvement in irrigation, new seeds, chemical fertilizers and herbicides, rice production increased to self-sufficiency levels in normal years. A boon to the technocrats in the 1970s was the high oil price, which enabled Indonesia, as a major exporter, to reap unexpected profits (though some of these were lost to the corrupt management of the national oil company). When oil prices fell in the 1980s, the government encouraged exports of other raw materials (lumber and minerals) and of industrial products manufactured by low-paid labour. In the 1990s, nearly all raw material prices were depressed, and there was strong competition for industrial investment from extreme low-cost producers like the People's Republic of China and Vietnam, which had been open to foreign investors since the mid-1980s.

Under the New Order, as the period after 1965 was called, Jakarta, like Singapore, had glittering high-rise office buildings and hotels, shopping centres and traffic jams. It also had an unequal share of national industry and wealth, and was bloated by immigrants from the hinterland (Singapore was fortunate to have no hinterland and it limited immigration). Java's intensive agriculture received priority from development planners, but other farmers, including producers for export, fared less well. The Outer Islands were, to policy-makers, sources of raw materials or sites for transmigration projects transferring people from overcrowded islands like Java, Bali and Madura.

In March 1998, Suharto, by then president for thirty years, stood successfully for another term of office, taking a close associate, B.J. Habibie, as his vice-president. Much of the 1998 rice crop was ruined by an exceptionally long dry season in 1997 (part of the worldwide disruption of weather patterns associated with the periodic warm Pacific current El Niño), while Sumatra and Kalimantan (Indonesian Borneo) were blanketed by smog from forest fires that spread to neighbouring countries. The fires were caused partly by the weather and partly by slash-and-burn farming, but they became so out of control because plantation owners had set them

Jakarta's vibrant commercial centres, high-rise buildings and traffic jams gave an illusion of wealth before the economic crisis of 1997–98. Ingrained problems such as irregularities in the banking system, unequal distribution of wealth, corruption and political uncertainty have prevented rapid recovery from the financial crash.

on a very large scale and the worked-over forest was no match for their incendiary methods of land-clearing.

Suharto had over years given family members and businessmen cronies, many of them from the Chinese minority, lucrative monopolies and other favours. Seeing the president as the root of the troubles, thousands of students and other demonstrators in May 1998 demanded his removal and punishment. The Indonesian currency, the rupiah, fell to an all-time low as capital flight and insolvency mounted, and Indonesia became hardest hit of all Asian countries in the financial crisis of 1997–98. Runaway inflation and shortages of necessities led to widespread scapegoating of ethnic Chinese and assaults on property. In brutal attacks on Jakarta's old Chinatown in May 1998, the demonstrators and other elements, probably linked to some military officers, burned, plundered and raped. The number of deaths reached 1,200 before Suharto stepped down, making way for Vice-President Habibie's succession.

Habibie promised reform and open elections. Student demonstrations continued, however, demanding that Suharto's family be called to account. They also pressured political leaders for a more rapid transition to political democracy and an accounting for human rights abuses. Conflict between Islamic and non-Islamic elements looms, and ethnic violence has recurred, some of it religiously motivated. Political tensions and ingrained loyalties stood in the way of economic reform and recovery. Indonesia's first free elections since 1955 were held in 1999, but whether the students and other reformist elements can help realize a working democracy (and what they mean by democracy) remains open.

The 1997 parliamentary elections in Indonesia, easily won by the government's Golkar, aroused strong opposition among some young people. Here, in May 1997, rioters clash with well-armed police. Violent riots in Jakarta and repeated demonstrations led by students helped to force President Suharto's resignation in May 1998.

## Malaysia

Malaysia abolished parliamentary democracy temporarily after Malay–Chinese riots in 1969, but resumed regular elections in 1972. The system was adjusted to ensure the political supremacy of Malays by tactics such as redefining electoral districts to give the ruling Malay party, UMNO, a strong majority in parliament. Between 1970 and 1990, the government implemented a New Economic Policy designed to put more economic control into Malay hands, at the expense of both foreigners and, to a lesser extent, Chinese, and to alleviate rural poverty, especially among Malays.

The core of the NEP was the transfer of share capital to Malays. Among other measures, the government established a number of foundations that held shares. Since these foundations were owned by and for Malays, this in effect transferred share capital to Malays. In some cases, these foundations simply bought out non-Malay interests in existing firms, hardly a case of Malay entrepreneurship. A new class of Malay businessmen grew up on the basis of privileged access to political influence, though this did not dampen the regard in which they were held by other Malays, who accepted inefficiencies and irregularities as the price for Malay economic control.

By the 1990s, Malaysia was no longer a mine-and-plantation economy but one built on a range of industries and export products. Many new opportunities have opened for Malays in education and industry, outside of their traditional occupations in government service and agriculture. Malaysia's prime minister since 1981, Dr Mahathir Mohammed, both led and profited from these changes. A champion of Malay interests and an abrasive spokesman for 'Asian

The world's tallest buildings, the Petronas Towers in Kuala Lumpur. Belonging to the national oil company, these skyscrapers symbolize Malaysia's determination to compete with Western nations in modernization and development.

values' and against Western cultures, Mahathir moved Malaysian government in a more authoritarian direction, but survived repeated challenges to his leadership over eighteen years.

Since the late 1980s, Malaysia's annual economic growth has averaged over 8 per cent, making it too one of the region's 'tiny tigers'. Mahathir has favoured highly visible development projects such as high-rise buildings, a 'national' car or the planned Multimedia Super Corridor (MSC), an Asian Silicon Valley. The 1997–98 economic crisis called these costly proposals into question. Mahathir adopted currency regulations and lowered interest rates to contain the immediate threat, and by 1999 economic turmoil was subsiding. Some controls were relaxed, but banking and financial reforms requested by the international community were never implemented.

These responses to the crisis led to a break between Mahathir and his long-time associate and 'crown prince', Deputy Premier Anwar Ibrahim, who favoured postponing expensive development projects. On the strength of what were probably poison-pen letters, Anwar was forced to resign and charged with corruption and sex offences, which under Malaysia's Islamic law carry heavy penalties. Pro-Anwar demonstrators founded a new opposition party. Even in alliance with the more conservative PAS (Partai Islam Se-Malaysia or Pan-Malaysian Islamic Party), the reform group faces no easy task.

### Thailand

Demonstrations for democracy in the 1970s failed to produce lasting change, but they were not futile. In 1980 the former General Prem Tinsulanonda became prime minister. A confidant of the king, Prem was a moderate and considered to be free of corruption, and was supported by a broad coalition in parliament. When Young Turks from the military attempted a coup against him in 1981, King Bhumibol, no longer a figurehead but a political actor, opted to support Prem, and in 1983 he confirmed the mandate. Prem held office until an elected successor replaced him in 1988. Thais called their government a Prem-ocracy.

Thailand's economic growth from the mid-1980s, making good use of the comparatively well-integrated local Chinese minority and drawing investments especially from Japan, surpassed that under the military dictators. Per capita income grew at a sustained rate of about 8 per cent; it too was a tiger economy. The structure of the economy changed: agriculture had generated 30 per cent of national income in 1970; by the 1990s this had dropped to 12 per cent.

Prem's successor was corrupt and unpopular. When the military staged a coup in 1991, installing a civilian caretaker, the move was widely applauded. Money politics had undermined elections and public policies. The votes of the two-thirds of Thais living in rural areas often overrode those of Bangkok, which was disadvantaged by the electoral system. Vote-buying was rampant in the countryside, as wealthy businessmen with few local interests purchased rural votes, and with them, political power in Bangkok.

After elections in 1992, Suchinda, a general who had once promised he would not become prime minister, decided to take that office. When protest demonstrations gripped Bangkok in May 1992 Suchinda responded with violence, but the military finally relented, making way for an elected civilian prime minister, Chuan Leekpai.

Forced to resign by a corruption scandal involving a colleague, Chuan gave way to new elections. Dominated by politicians with business connections, these were a triumph of money politics. The government mishandled the financial crisis of 1997, making it worse. Public outcry and demonstrations forced the incumbent prime minister to resign. His replacement, heading a coalition cabinet, was the competent and personally honest former prime minister, Chuan Leekpai, who presided over the beginning recovery.

In all these changes, Thailand's new middle class seems to have seized the political initiative. Thai society has been transformed irrevocably since early postwar days, but enormous problems remain. It has a serious regional imbalance, with Bangkok alone producing half of national wealth. A sluggish bureaucracy treats citizens with paternalistic immobility. Country people continue to move to Bangkok, exacerbating urban sprawl. Some 250,000 children are involved in prostitution, according to one estimate. Democracy, in spite of the adoption of a new constitution in 1997, may well continue to be corrupted by money politics.

More significant than the fact of Chuan Leekpai's return, however, was the behaviour of the military. In a situation of uncertainty that a decade before would have seemed to cry out for intervention, the soldiers remained in their barracks. Whether democracy is on the right track or not, it seems coup days are over.

The winning smile of Thailand's Prime Minister Chuan Leekpai. Chuan had led a coalition to power in 1994, but resigned after a scandal. The Thais turned to him again when the reigning government bungled the handling of the economic crisis of 1997, which began in Bangkok and soon spread through Southeast Asia and parts of East Asia.

173

Troops moving through Rangoon shortly after the army retook control of the country in 1962 under General Ne Win, a control that it has retained to this day.

## Burma

In 1962 the army (Tatmadaw) assumed power under the leadership of General U Ne Win, once one of Aung San's Thirty Comrades (see p. 132). Political leaders and prominent journalists were imprisoned. 'The Burmese Way to Socialism' was offered as ideological underpinning for a military dictatorship that was meant to be long-term, and the military governed with a heavy hand. The nation virtually reverted to its precolonial status as 'hermit kingdom', as outsiders, journalists and even Burmese who had lived abroad for a long time were denied entry. This deliberate policy of isolation also entailed a divorce from the world economy. Industries still privately owned were nationalized or closely supervised, and the government took over the distribution of essential commodities. Retailing, importing and exporting, and manufacturing no longer offered opportunities to remaining Indian and Chinese minorities. Excruciatingly slow growth and a general decline in trade accompanied widespread poverty, while much trade diverted to the black market.

Renting agricultural land to tenants was made illegal in 1965. The state henceforth determined land use and set production quotas through local committees, as well as purchasing rice, still Burma's most important crop, at controlled prices. Rice production stagnated

in the 1960s and 1970s, Burma's export earnings declined, and some areas experienced serious shortages. Rebellious minorities in border areas were in control of some of the most profitable mineral-producing regions. In 1974, Ne Win, increasingly unpopular, announced his withdrawal from the government. On paper, a new constitution provided for a parliament and the separation of powers, but in practice Ne Win continued to exercise power from behind the scenes.

In the 1980s, the government began to invest in agricultural improvement, and at the same time created limited opportunities for foreign investment, particularly in petroleum and raw material exploitation, or in tourism and hotels, where investors from Singapore and Malaysia have been especially active. A series of 'standfast' (ceasefire) agreements appeared to promise an end to conflicts with minority groups, although thousands of refugees, most of them Muslims from the western state of Arakan, remained in Bangladesh, and other minorities sought refuge along the border with Thailand. Another rebellious group, the Communist Party of Burma, had all but eliminated itself by a series of bloody purges of its leadership during the Chinese Cultural Revolution of the late 1960s.

Of all ethnic groups fighting the government of Burma, the Karen have been among the most determined. Here young soldiers, some mere boys, present their weapons for inspection at a rebel base in Karen-controlled territory.

In 1988, widespread protests involving students, monks and others broke out in Burma and threatened military rule. Lasting from March to September, the demonstrations brought the 'resignation' of General Ne Win, but were in the end brutally suppressed by the military.

Dissatisfaction could not be expressed in the controlled press, and on 12 March 1988 there began a series of peaceful, student-led but widely supported demonstrations. Apart from students demanding an end to military dictatorship, many monks participated to urge an end to central jurisdiction over the sangha, which the military had enforced in 1980. The government and cooperating ecclesiastics had registered monks, imposed restrictions on their public behaviour, and interfered in internal sangha matters.

After an attempt to suppress the demonstrations, Ne Win again 'resigned' in July. Protests continued, despite brutal military and police intervention against the demonstrators, until August 1988. In that month, thousands of convicted criminals escaped or were released from jail, possibly as a threat to the demonstrators. Thousands of dissidents and supporters of opposition parties were subsequently arrested to take their places in jail. By September, military repression had prevailed.

In September 1988 the army named new successors to power, a junta called the 'State Law and Order Restoration Council' (SLORC), with General Saw Maung as its head and Brigadier General Khin Nyunt as a crucial link to the still-powerful Ne Win. Many young people fled to the border areas or into Thailand; some tried to link up with minority peoples' rebellions but found their goals and lifestyles incompatible, while both the jungle and the Thai government proved inhospitable. As the army attacked the minority rebels with renewed force and brutality, some agreed to truces, while many students returned to Burma under a probably specious amnesty offer.

Not long after the repression of the demonstrators, the ruling SLORC unexpectedly abolished the army-led Burma Socialist Programme Party, the only legal party in existence, dissolved parliament and announced that it now favoured a multi-party system. Elections were scheduled for 1990 for a parliament called the People's Assembly.

The return of Aung San's daughter Aung San Suu Kyi from abroad to care for her dying mother in late 1988 had attracted considerable public attention. With political parties suddenly legalized she joined with others to form a National League for Democracy (NLD). Many other parties blossomed, and the army itself entered the scene with a reconstructed Burma Socialist Programme Party called the National Unity Party.

In the event, the National League for Democracy, with Aung San Suu Kyi as its secretary-general, won 82 per cent of the constituencies. But it was never permitted to take its seats. The SLORC had probably agreed to hold elections because foreign powers, including the USA, Japan and European states, had withdrawn aid and boycotted trade after the brutal repression of 1988. The elections were intended to demonstrate an openness to democracy. Instead, party leaders were imprisoned and Aung San Suu Kyi placed under house arrest.

SLORC announced that, before parliament could convene, there must be a National Convention to write a new constitution. Political parties were a minority in this body even before 86 NLD delegates were expelled in 1995. Although foreign pleading achieved some improvement of the conditions under which Suu Kyi was being kept, other democratic leaders languished or died in captivity, and the army continued to hold to its anti-democratic course. A change in name, from SLORC to State Peace and Development Council, had little effect on military habits of domination or on Ne Win's still decisive role. Also changed was the name of the country, with the adoption of Myanmar, the Burmese pronunciation of 'Burma', and the new spelling of Yangon for the capital Rangoon.

Meanwhile, the military leadership attempted to attract foreign capital without changing its political stripes. Western countries, however, have imposed investment boycotts on Burma so long as current policies prevail; since 1988 the World Bank has refused it credit. In 1997, ASEAN attempted to break the impasse by admitting Burma/Myanmar to membership; members spoke about 'constructive engagement'. This decision has marred ASEAN relations with Western countries, the latter still intent on imposing international isolation on Burma's military rulers, and has had no noticeable effect on the country's internal politics.

Aung San Suu Kyi, daughter of Burma's nationalist hero Aung San, has become the symbol of Burma's democratic opposition. She led the National League for Democracy to an overwhelming majority in elections of 1990, but the party was never allowed to take power and she has been under house arrest ever since.

## Vietnam

Economic liberalization, which affected most Southeast Asian countries to some extent in the 1960s and 1970s, finally reached Vietnam in the 1980s. The first years after 1975 had been extremely difficult, as the legacies of war and destruction took their toll, while the imposition of socialism on southern Vietnam's capitalist-tinged industry and agriculture brought that economy to collapse. Those accused of collaboration with the pro-American regimes were arrested, while hundreds of thousands of refugees fled the country.

At the end of 1978, Vietnam invaded Cambodia, putting an end to the Khmer Rouge rule of terror there, but in turn provoking a war with China on the northern border; China probably meant to aid the Khmer Rouge by diverting Vietnamese forces. Because of hostilities with China and stricter regulation of small private enterprises in the north, some 700,000 ethnic Chinese, nearly 200,000 from the north, left the country between 1978 and 1982. Vietnam became almost totally dependent on the Soviet Union for aid and imports, and thousands of Vietnamese guest workers left for Eastern European countries. In 1988, some northern provinces were touched by a famine that was exacerbated by bureaucratic bungling.

Because of mounting economic difficulties, in 1986 the Sixth Party Congress of the Vietnam Workers' Party determined to emphasize agriculture and to give freer rein to other parts of the economy, a policy known as *doi moi*. Vietnam now experiments with export-oriented production, and encourages tourists and other foreign visitors. However, foreign investments are only welcome in

After years of meagre rations, the Vietnamese began to enjoy better-filled rice bowls in the 1990s. This harvest being transported by ox-cart promises an end to shortages.

Economic liberalization – *doi moi* – has brought opportunities for some foreign investors in Vietnam's industries. Here in Ho Chi Minh City (formerly Saigon) factory workers assemble a vehicle.

a restricted framework. Rapid growth of the market has brought uneven rewards; poverty persists, especially in rural areas and among the hill peoples that constitute the country's ethnic minorities.

The partial opening of the socialist economy under *doi moi* did not mean a loosening of the party's grip on political power; unlike in the USSR, Vietnam's economic opening was not accompanied by political liberalization. On the contrary, leaders repeatedly confirmed the party's rule over both government and the economy in accordance with Marxist–Leninist ideology. In state and party, the old leaders who had fought side by side with Ho Chi Minh since the 1940s have given way to successor generations. Relations with China have been mended; a vigorous border trade takes place in the north. The 1995 admission to ASEAN and subsequent exchange of diplomatic relations with the USA stand out as key moments in Vietnam's carefully orchestrated international opening.

### Cambodia and Laos

The Khmer Rouge, as the Communist Party of Kampuchea continues to be known, implemented between April 1975 and December 1978 a social revolution in Cambodia that left no institution or social grouping intact and at least half a million – some estimate many more – Cambodians dead. Under Pol Pot (a pseudonym for Saloth Sar, 1928–98), a Khmer who had become enamoured of Marxism and then Maoism while studying in Paris, the Khmer Rouge closed off the country to the outside world and embarked on a radical reconstruction of society. In Democratic Kampuchea (as they renamed Cambodia) the royal court was abolished, schools and monasteries emptied and cities evacuated, their populations

Pol Pot, the nom de guerre of the Khmer Rouge leader responsible for an unparalleled reign of terror in Cambodia, and for violent opposition after he was driven from power, died unreconciled and unrepentant in the Cambodian jungle in 1998.

herded into the countryside to work in huge agricultural cooperatives. Families were driven apart and intellectuals murdered en masse. Horrible relics of imprisonment, torture and death are still kept in Tuol Sleng prison in Phnom Penh.

Provoked by border incidents, the Khmer Rouge's increasing xenophobia and the elimination of Khmer Communists sympathetic to Vietnam, Vietnamese troops invaded Cambodia in December 1978, quickly overrunning most of the country. The Vietnamese installed Hun Sen as prime minister of the People's Republic of Kampuchea and guaranteed most Khmer a time of peace to recover from terror and disruption. In the eyes of most of the world, and of many Khmer who fled abroad, this represented no more than a Vietnamese colonization of the country. Western countries and the United Nations refused diplomatic recognition to the People's Republic of Kampuchea, and Khmer Rouge representatives continued, for example, to sit in the United Nations. The new regime failed to suppress Khmer Rouge elements, who continued to occupy rural bases, especially along the Thai border. Meanwhile, another, pro-royalist force coalesced around former head of state Prince Sihanouk, who had withdrawn to Beijing and North Korea after the invasion. Three armed groups competed for power in the small and devastated country.

UN intervention finally organized negotiations in Paris in 1991 in an attempt to bring the three competing elements together and secure some kind of peace. In 1993, elections brought a coalition

A gruesome memorial to the hundreds of thousands – perhaps millions – of victims of Khmer Rouge terror in Cambodia (then Kampuchea) between 1975 and 1978.

government into being, under co-premiers Hun Sen of the Cambodian People's Party and Prince Ranariddh, a son of Sihanouk, representing the royalist Funcinpec faction. The Khmer Rouge refused to recognize the election results (in which they had done badly) and some fighting continued. In 1997, fighting broke out between supporters of the two premiers, and in June that year Hun Sen launched a coup against Ranariddh, forcing the prince into exile. Elections in 1998 were, by agreement, to choose a single premier. Hun Sen went to work intimidating or assassinating opponents in order to ensure his victory, but Ranariddh returned to the country to campaign shortly before the voting. The election confirmed Hun Sen as premier, although it was challenged from various sides. In a footnote to the struggles, Pol Pot himself, ill with malaria and other ailments from his years in the jungle, died shortly before the elections.

While Hun Sen's coup led ASEAN members to postpone the admission of Cambodia until 1999, the Lao People's Democratic Republic (together with Burma) was admitted to full membership in 1997. Although in Laos the Communist party, called the Lao People's Revolutionary Party, retains its monopoly of political power, this tiny country has already been swept up with the tide of international opening. Not only has international aid and investment grown, but so has tourism: between 1990 and 1996 the number of visitors to Laos increased from 14,000 to 403,000, with Thais greatly outnumbering Western visitors.

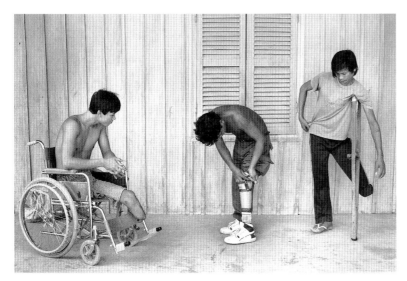

Cambodia's living also bear the scars of terror and war. Large areas of the country were mined in the fighting between Khmer Rouge and other factions, and these young people have lost limbs to landmine explosions. Although charitable organizations exist to provide artificial limbs, many victims are too impoverished to spend the weeks, sometimes months, it takes to have them fitted properly.

## ASEAN

Five nations – Indonesia, Malaysia, the Philippines, Singapore and Thailand – formed the Association of Southeast Asian Nations in 1967. Although their original intention was to reduce the level of tension in the region by means of frequent consultations, especially after the Indonesian hostilities against Malaysia and Singapore in 1963–66 (see p. 156), this loose association soon expanded its role and took on new members. When, in 1975–78, hundreds of thousands of refugees fled the Indochina countries for Thailand, Malaysia and Indonesia, ASEAN was able to pressure other, mostly Western, countries to accept them after they had been temporarily housed in Southeast Asian camps. The organization has also been able to represent common interests to trading and political partners like Japan, the USA, China and the European Union and has begun to make cautious steps toward more mutual free trade and travel.

Brunei became the sixth member of the association on achieving independence in 1984. In the 1990s, ASEAN made the decision to expand in order to represent all Southeast Asia, accepting first Vietnam, then Burma and Laos, and finally Cambodia, to membership.

Despite its tradition of cooperation and consultation, the organization seemed to fall silent in the economic crisis of 1997–98, and it was ineffective in meeting the consequences of the economic troubles. Its 1998 meeting opened other rifts, as some member states, which themselves had introduced democracy in the 1980s and 1990s, began to speak openly of the need to discuss human rights issues among ASEAN members, even if this broke the taboo against interference in each other's affairs. Furthermore, unlike the original five states, the new members are no 'tiger economies'. Instead, they are among the world's poorest nations. ASEAN is now more representative of Southeast Asians but the per capita income of the group has fallen greatly through the inclusion of new states. The expansion of the organization may, in the end, increase internal tensions in what was once a courteous but not terribly decisive club.

## THE ENVIRONMENT

Among the many challenges to environmental preservation in Southeast Asia are urban traffic and its resulting air pollution, untreated human and industrial wastes, the problem of access to clean water, energy conservation, use of dangerous chemicals in agriculture and industry, and – perhaps the most intractable – preservation of the tropical forest. Up to now, governments have shown limited resolve in meeting these challenges, and the problems continue to mount. Southeast Asia's natural bounty and lush vegetation seemed for centuries to promise never-ending plenty; now that population growth has depleted and threatened resources, attitudes are slow to change.

The damage done to the region's forests in the past three or four decades has been dramatic, and is past repair. In the 1930s, three-quarters of Thailand was covered with forest; by 1985 it was one-third, and still declining. SLORC has allowed Burma's forests to be exploited by interests from Thailand in order to raise cash. A similar process is under way in Cambodia, where the Khmer Rouge traded resources for weapons and supplies to maintain its struggle against Hun Sen.

Java's forest all but disappeared in colonial times: its great teak trees were cut down to build ships for the VOC and houses for well-to-do urbanites, while the peasants cut wood for their own use or cleared forest simply to open agricultural lands. The decimation of forests in Sumatra and Kalimantan, however, is part of the forced development process pursued by Suharto since 1966. Great, irreplaceable trees have often been felled for mere plywood and replanting has never fulfilled prescribed quotas. Instead, deforestation opened the way for settlers, both officially sanctioned and so-called 'spontaneous' migrants, who soon began farming and made any reforestation impossible. The effects can be seen in the muddy rivers that once ran clear and in the increased tendency to flooding, as well as in repeated smogs from burning forests (the acrid smoke of 1997

Young boys propel a boat through a landscape of urban refuse. Southeast Asia's giant metropolises produce mountains of garbage and industrial waste; few dispose of it adequately.

183

Malaysians attempt to avoid severe smog pollution by wearing masks in 1997, when large areas of Southeast Asia were smothered in a grey acrid haze. Deforestation and clearing by fire in a dry year caused uncontrollable burning over huge areas of forest in parts of Indonesia and Malaysian Borneo.

was not the first of its kind). In addition, many observers believe climate changes, particularly the extreme dry seasons experienced in recent years, are an effect of the destruction of forest cover. Apart from climatic and ecological effects, deforestation directly threatens the way of life of forest-dwelling minorities, who depend on forest products for their existence. It also may destroy valuable non-timber resources like rare plants and animals.

Singapore has tackled the traffic and pollution problem by limiting vehicle admission to the inner city and pricing automobiles out of the reach of average citizens. It has also built up a public transport system, including a modern metro. With its limited population, it can implement campaigns to restrict population growth, energy waste, or water use without resistance from competing interests emanating from agriculture and forestry – like Japan, it builds while others fell.

Maritime Southeast Asia is also experiencing depletion of ocean resources through overfishing, including fishing by foreign, industrial vessels, and through use of destructive methods by local people. Pollution contributes to the reduction of catches in some areas, or to making them inedible.

Some of the Southeast Asian middle classes have not limited their interests to television sets, karaoke and mobile phones. Just as some, in countries like Indonesia, Thailand and the Philippines, have pressed for more democratic and accountable government, others have formed non-government organizations concerned with promoting human rights, aiding the oppressed, or protecting the environment. Such activities are a ray of hope, if perhaps only a pale one, to observers who regard political leaders as incapable of decisive action. What is feasible in times of economic growth and optimism is less so in more straitened circumstances, and while some countries seem to be slowly recovering from the economic crisis of 1997–98, the prospects for Indonesia are uncertain. It therefore remains to be seen whether environmentalist and human rights groups will succeed in convincing others to revise their policies and their personal choices.

# GLOSSARY

**asrama** – a residential school

**bodhisattva** – in Mahayana Buddhism, one of the enlightened who does not enter Nirvana but remains in contact with earthly beings and helps them attain enlightenment

**candi** – temple

**chakravartin** – ruler 'who turns the wheel of the universe'; title of Southeast Asian rulers

**dakwah** – preaching, movement to reawaken Islamic fervour

**dao** – 'the way'; the principle of Taoism or Daoism

**dewaraja** – literally 'god-king' or 'king of the gods'; a title of early Southeast Asian rulers

**dharma** – the law, especially Buddhist law

**jihad** – Islamic holy war

**kapitan** – the headman of an ethnic minority community, especially Chinese (from the Portuguese for captain)

**kaum muda** – 'the young ones'; modernists, especially with reference to Islam

**kaum tua** – 'the old ones'; traditionalists, especially with reference to Islam

**kiai** – title of an Islamic scholar, especially in Java

**kris** – a Malay or Indonesian dagger with a typical wavy blade

**linga** – phallus, symbol of male power especially identified with the god Siva

**madrasah** – traditional Islamic school

**Mahdi** – the coming prophet, a messianic figure in some Islamic traditions

**Maitreya** – the Buddha whose birth signals a new era, a millenarian figure

**mandala** – a geometric figure that concentrates spiritual energy in the centre; also used to describe a political constellation with a dominant centre and a number of subordinate polities

**naga** – serpent

**negara** – city, especially in the sense of royal city, or a nation

**orang laut** – literally 'people of the sea'; boat-dwelling peoples of the Malayan Peninsula and Indonesian Archipelago, sometimes called 'sea nomads'

**perang sabil** – Indonesian/Malay equivalent of **jihad**

**pesantren** – traditional Islamic rural schools, especially in Java, now often modernized

**Pinyin** – Beijing standard orthography for transliteration of Mandarin Chinese

**ratu adil** – 'just king'; a messianic figure in Javanese and Indonesian tradition

**reformasi** – 'reform'; in Indonesia and Malaysia used especially to mean greater democracy and respect for human rights

**romusha** – members of labour battalions recruited by the Japanese in occupied countries during World War II

**sangha** – the institution of the Buddhist monkhood

**stupa** – a Buddhist temple, usually more or less bell-shaped

**tantra** – holy texts of Tantric Buddhism, which uses esoteric devices to attain enlightenment

**ulama** – Islamic scholars

**wat** – temple

**wayang** – literally 'shadow'; shadow-puppet theatre, particularly used in Java (**wayang kulit**); also used to mean puppet and dance theatre derived from the shadow plays

**yoni** – female sexual symbol

# SHORT BIBLIOGRAPHY

Emphasis is on widely available literature and basic histories. Items listed under one chapter may also be of interest for later periods.

## GENERAL

Bernhard Dahm and Roderich Ptak (eds), *Südostasien Handbuch: Geschichte, Gesellschaft, Politik, Wirtschaft, Kultur* (Munich: C.H. Beck, 1999)

Milton Osborne, *Southeast Asia: An Introductory History* (St Leonards NSW: Allen and Unwin, 1995)

Nicholas Tarling (ed.), *The Cambridge History of Southeast Asia* (Cambridge: Cambridge University Press, 1992): Vol. I, *From Early Times to c. 1800*; Vol. II, *The Nineteenth and Twentieth Centuries*

O.W. Wolters, *History, Culture, and Region in Southeast Asian Perspectives* (Singapore: Institute of Southeast Asian Studies, 1982)

## HISTORIES OF INDIVIDUAL COUNTRIES

David P. Chandler, *A History of Cambodia* (Boulder: Westview Press, 1983)

Denys Lombard, *Le Carrefour javanais: essai d'histoire globale* (Paris: Éditions de l'École des Hautes Études en Sciences Sociales, 1990): Vol. 1, *Les Limites de l'occidentalisation*; Vol. 2 *Les Réseaux asiatiques*; Vol. 3, *L'Héritage des royaumes concentriques*

M.C. Ricklefs, *A History of Modern Indonesia c. 1300 to the Present* (Bloomington: Indiana University Press, 1981)

Keith W. Taylor, *The Birth of Vietnam* (Berkeley: University of California Press, 1983)

Robert H. Taylor, *The State in Burma* (Honolulu: University of Hawaii Press and London: C. Hurst and Co., 1987)

David J. Steinberg, *The Philippines: A Singular and a Plural Place* (Boulder, CO and Oxford: Westview Press, 1994)

Martin Stuart-Fox, *A History of Laos* (Cambridge: Cambridge University Press, 1997)

C.M. Turnbull, *A History of Singapore 1819–1975* (Kuala Lumpur: Oxford University Press, 1977)

Barbara Watson Andaya and Leonard Y. Andaya, *A History of Malaysia* (London and Basingstoke: Macmillan, 1982)

David K. Wyatt, *Thailand: A Short History* (New Haven: Yale University Press, 1984)

## Chapter One
**Waterways**
*From Early Settlements to the First Maritime Kingdoms*

A.J. Bernet Kempers, *The Kettledrums of Southeast Asia: A Bronze Age World and its Aftermath (Modern Quaternary Research in Southeast Asia,* Vol. 10, 1986–87) (Rotterdam and Brookfield: A.A. Balkema, 1988)

G. Coedès, *The Indianized States of Southeast Asia,* ed. by Walter F. Vella, tr. by Susan Brown Cowing (Honolulu: The University Press of Hawaii, 1968)

G. Coedès, *The Making of South East Asia* (Berkeley: University of California Press, 1969)

Arne and Eva Eggebrecht (eds), *Versuknene Königreiche Indonesiens* (Mainz: von Zabern, 1995), exhibition catalogue, Roemer- und Pelizaeus Museum, Hildesheim

Kenneth Hall, *Maritime Trade and State Development in Early Southeast Asia* (Honolulu: University of Hawaii Press, 1985)

Charles Higham, *The Archaeology of Mainland Southeast Asia: from 10,000 BC to the Fall of Angkor* (Cambridge: Cambridge University Press, 1989)

Charles Higham, *The Bronze Age of Southeast Asia* (Cambridge: Cambridge University Press, 1996)

R.B. Smith and W. Watson (eds),

*Early South East Asia: Essays in Archaeology, History and Historical Geography* (New York and Kuala Lumpur: Oxford University Press, 1979)

Paul Wheatley, *The Golden Khersonese: Studies in the Historical Geography of the Malay Peninsula before AD 1500* (Kuala Lumpur: Penerbit Universiti Malaya, 1960, repr. 1980)

O.W. Wolters, *Early Indonesian Commerce: A Study of the Origins of Srivijaya* (Ithaca: Cornell University Press, 1967)

O.W. Wolters, *The Fall of Srivijaya in Malay History* (Ithaca: Cornell University Press, 1970)

## Chapter Two
**Temples and Rice**
*Land-Based Kingdoms*

Michael Aung-Thwin, *Pagan: The Origins of Modern Burma* (Honolulu: University of Hawaii Press, 1985)

Madeleine Giteau, *Histoire d'Angkor* (Paris and Pondicherry: Kailash Editions, 1996)

Helen Ibbitson Jessup and Thierry Zephir (eds), *Sculpture of Angkor and Ancient Cambodia: Millennium of Glory* (New York and London: Thames & Hudson, 1997)

Ian Mabbett and David Chandler, *The Khmers* (*The Peoples of South-East Asia and the Pacific*) (Oxford and Cambridge MA: Blackwell Publishers, 1995)

David G. Marr and A.C. Milner (eds), *Southeast Asia in the 9th to 14th Centuries* (Singapore: Institute of Southeast Asian Studies and Canberra: Research School of Pacific Studies, Australian National University, 1986)

John Miksic, *Borobudur: Golden Tales of the Buddhas* (Berkeley: Periplus Editions, 1990)

John Miksic, *Ancient History* (Indonesian Heritage Series, Vol. 1) (Singapore: Archipelago Press, Editions Didier Millet, 1996)

Paul Wheatley, *Nagara and Commandery: Origins of the Southeast*

*Asian Urban Traditions* (Chicago: The University of Chicago Department of Geography, 1983: research paper nos 207–08, double number)

## Chapter Three
**Multiplicity of Beliefs**
*The Religions of Southeast Asia*

Ahmad Ibrahim, Sharon Siddique and Yasmin Hussain (eds), *Readings on Islam in Southeast Asia* (Singapore: Institute of Southeast Asian Studies, 1985)

Charles F. Keyes, *The Golden Peninsula: Culture and Adaptation in Mainland Southeast Asia* (New York: Macmillan, 1977, repr. Honolulu: University of Hawaii Press, 1995)

Hue Tam Ho Tai, *Millenarianism and Peasant Politics in Vietnam* (Cambridge MA and London: Harvard University Press, 1983)

S.J. Tambiah, *World Conqueror and World Renouncer: A Study of Buddhism and Polity in Thailand against a Historical Background* (Cambridge: Cambridge University Press, 1976)

## Chapter Four
**Southeast Asia as a Crossroads**
*Relations with China and European Advances*

Leonard Blussé, *Strange Company: Chinese Settlers, Mestizo Women and the Dutch in VOC Batavia* (Dordrecht: Foris Publications, 1986)

Anthony Reid (ed.), *Early Modern History* (Indonesian Heritage Series, Vol. 3) (Singapore: Archipelago Press, Editions Didier Miller, 1996)

Anthony Reid, *Southeast Asia in the Age of Commerce, 1450–1680*: Vol. I, *The Lands Below the Winds* (New Haven: Yale University Press, 1988); Vol. II, *Expansion and Crisis* (New Haven: Yale University Press, 1993)

Li Tana, *Nguyen Cochinchina: Southern Vietnam in the Seventeenth and Eighteenth Centuries* (Ithaca NY:

Cornell Southeast Asia Program, 1998)

Jean Taylor, *The Social World of Batavia: European and Eurasian in Dutch Asia* (Madison: University of Wisconsin Press, 1983)

Alexander B. Woodside, *Vietnam and the Chinese Model* (Cambridge MA: Harvard University Press, 1971)

## CHAPTER FIVE
## New Directions, New Elites
### *The Colonial Map of Southeast Asia*

Michael Adas, *The Burma Delta* (Madison: University of Wisconsin Press, 1974)

Benedict Anderson, *Imagined Communities: Reflections on the Origin and Spread of Nationalism* (London: Verso Editions, 1983)

Ann Booth, *The Indonesian Economy in the Nineteenth and Twentieth Centuries: A History of Missed Opportunities* (London: Macmillan Press and New York: St Martin's Press, 1998)

Pierre Brocheux, *The Mekong Delta: Ecology, Economy, and Revolution, 1860–1960* (Madison: University of Wisconsin, Center for Southeast Asian Studies, 1995)

Bernhard Dahm, *Sukarno's Struggle for Indonesian Independence*, tr. by Mary F. Somers Heidhues (Ithaca, New York: Cornell University Press, 1969)

R.E. Elson, *The End of the Peasantry in Southeast Asia: A Social and Economic History of Peasant Livelihood, 1800–1990s* (Houndmills, Basingstoke, Hampshire and London: Macmillan Press, 1997)

Ruth T. McVey, *The Rise of Indonesian Communism* (Ithaca: Cornell University Press, 1965)

David G. Marr, *Vietnamese Anticolonialism 1885–1925* (Berkeley: University of California Press, 1971)

David G. Marr, *Vietnamese Tradition on Trial, 1920–1945* (Berkeley: University of California Press, 1981)

James C. Scott, *The Moral Economy of the Peasant: Rebellion and Subsistence in Southeast Asia* (New Haven: Yale University Press, 1976)

Takashi Shiraishi, *An Age in Motion: Popular Radicalism in Java, 1912–1926* (Ithaca: Cornell University Press, 1990)

## CHAPTER SIX
## Violence and Transition
### *Occupation, Independence and Cold War*

Robert Cribb and Colin Brown, *Modern Indonesia: A History Since 1945* (London and New York: Longman, 1995)

Harold Crouch, *The Army and Politics in Indonesia (Politics and International Relations of Southeast Asia*, gen. ed. George McT. Kahin) (Ithaca: Cornell University Press, 1978)

William J. Duiker, *The Communist Road to Power in Vietnam* (Boulder CO: Westview Press, 1996)

Herbert Feith, *The Decline of Constitutional Democracy in Indonesia* (Ithaca: Cornell University Press, 1962)

George McT. Kahin, *Nationalism and Revolution in Indonesia* (Ithaca: Cornell University Press, 1952)

Ben Kiernan, *The Pol Pot Regime: Race, Power, and Genocide in Cambodia under the Khmer Rouge, 1975–1979* (New Haven: Yale University Press, 1996)

Paul Kratoska, *The Japanese Occupation of Malaya 1941–1945* (London: C. Hurst and Honolulu: University of Hawaii Press, 1997)

David G. Marr, *Vietnam 1945: The Quest for Power* (Berkeley: University of California Press, 1995)

Anthony J.S. Reid, *The Indonesian National Revolution 1945–1950* (Hawthorn Victoria: Longman Australia, 1974)

William S. Turley, *The Second Indochina War: A Short Political and Military History 1954–1975* (Boulder CO: West View Press, 1986)

Alexander B. Woodside, *Community and Revolution in Modern Vietnam* (Boston: Houghton Mifflin, 1976)

## CHAPTER SEVEN
## Development and Democracy
### *Southeast Asia in Recent Decades*

John Girling, *Interpreting Development: Capitalism, Democracy, and the Middle Class in Thailand (Studies on Southeast Asia)* (Ithaca: Southeast Asia Program, Cornell University, 1996)

Kevin Hewison, Richard Robison and Garry Rodan (eds), *Southeast Asia in the 1990s: Authoritarianism, Democracy and Capitalism* (St Leonards NSW: Allen and Unwin, 1993)

James V. Jesudason, *Ethnicity and the Economy: The State, Chinese Business, and Multinationals in Malaysia* (Singapore: Oxford University Press, 1989)

Benedict J. Kerkvliet and Resil B. Mojares (eds), *From Marcos to Aquino: Local Perspectives on Political Transition in the Philippines* (Honolulu: University of Hawaii Press and Manila: Ateneo de Manila University Press, 1991)

Anek Laothamatas (ed.), *Democratization in Southeast and East Asia* (Singapore: Institute of Southeast Asian Studies and Bangkok: Silkworm Books, 1997)

R.S. Milne and Diane Mauzy, *Malaysian Politics under Mahathir* (London and New York: Routledge, 1999)

Gareth Porter, *Vietnam: The Politics of Bureaucratic Socialism* (Ithaca: Cornell University Press, 1993)

Douglas E. Ramage, *Politics in Indonesia: Democracy, Islam, and the Ideology of Tolerance* (London: Routledge, 1995)

Richard Robison, *Indonesia: The Rise of Capital* (Sydney: Allen and Unwin, 1986)

Adam Schwarz, *A Nation in Waiting: Indonesia in the 1990s* (St Leonards NSW: Allen and Unwin, 1994)

David Wurfel, *Filipino Politics: Development and Decay* (Quezon City: Ateneo de Manila University Press, 1991)

# ILLUSTRATION AND TEXT CREDITS

a = above, b = below, l = left,
r = right, c = centre

## SOURCES OF ILLUSTRATIONS

AKG London: 20, 47, 59, 139;
Koninklijk Instituut voor de Tropen,
Amsterdam: 21, 34, 37, 53, 54, 114,
120; Rijksinstituut voor
Oorlogsdocumentie, Amsterdam: 122;
Rijksmuseum, Amsterdam: 100;
Ancient Art & Architecture
Collection: 51(a), 87; Associated
Press: 151, 152; Collection of Prince
Chalermbol Yugala, Bangkok: 60;
Borneo Co.: 116(a), 116(b); Camera
Press: 44, 50(r), 72(a), 72(br) 74(l), 79,
83, 84, 86, 117(a), 141(r), 148(cl),
160, 162, 164, 165, 166, 167(l),
167(r), 168, 170, 172, 173, 175, 176,
177, 178, 179, 180(a), 180(b), 181,
184; Douglas Dickens: 48(a), 117(b);
118; e.t. archive: 27, 95, 104(a),
104(b), 146; Jack Garafolo: 33(b);
National Museum, Hanoi: 20(a);
Hulton Getty: 58: 64, 74(r), 88, 101,
108, 119, 127(b), 129, 130, 132, 133,
141(l), 142, 145, 148(a), 148(cr),
148(b), 153, 154(a); Indopix: 32,
50(l), 82; Institut Kern, Leiden: 23;
John Miksic: 55; Musée de l'Homme,
Paris: 38, 96; National Museum of
Phnom Penh: 41; Josephine Powell:
42, 48(b), 62; Roger-Viollet: 107(a),
107(b); Topham Picturepoint: 25, 40,
72(bl), 75, 127(a), 134, 136, 150,
154(b), 155, 157, 171, 183; British
Library, London: 70(a), 111; British
Museum, London: 98; Malaya House,
London: 158; Asian Art Museum of
San Francisco. The Avery Brundage
Collection: 2; Tara Sosrowardoyo,
*Indonesian Art: Treasures of the National
Museum*, Editions Didier Millet: 29,
30, 51(b); Loke Wan: 43(a); Werner
Forman Archive: 19, 33(a), 43(b), 66,
80, 90.

Maps were redrawn by Renuka
Madan after the following sources:
p. 17 after John Miksic ed., *Ancient
History* (Indonesian Heritage Series
Vol. 1) (Singapore: Archipelago Press,
Editions Didier Millet, 1996) p. 36;
p. 46 after Claire Holt, *Art in
Indonesia: Continuities and Change*
(Ithaca: Cornell University Press,
1966) p. 41; pp. 56–57 after Jan M.
Pluvier, *Historical Atlas of Southeast
Asia* (Leiden, New York, Cologne:
E.J. Brill, 1995) pp. 14–15; p. 78 after
Denys Lombard, *Le Carrefour javanais:
essai d'histoire globale* (Paris: Éditions de
l'École des Hautes Études en Sciences
Sociales, 1990) Vol. 3, *L'Héritage des
royaumes concentriques* p. 10; p. 94 after
Lê Thành Khôi, *Histoire du Viêt Nam
des origines à 1858* (Paris: sudestasie,
1992) p. 315; p. 140(l) King C. Chen,
*Vietnam and China, 1938–1954*
(Princeton: Princeton University
Press, 1969) p. 298.

## SOURCES OF QUOTATIONS

The Chinese traveller I Ching, cited
in G. Coedès, *The Indianized States
of Southeast Asia*, tr. by Susan Brown
Cowing (Honolulu: The University
Press of Hawaii, 1968) p. 81 (quoted
on p. 28); Telaga Batu inscription,
cited in John Miksic (ed.), *Ancient
History* (Indonesian Heritage Series
Vol. 1) (Singapore: Archipelago Press,
Editions Didier Millet,1996), p. 53
(quoted on p. 29); Ma Tuan-lin, cited
in Ian Mabbett and David Chandler,
*The Khmers* (Oxford: Blackwell,
1995), p. 85 (quoted on p. 37); the
procession of Hayam Wuruk
described by Mpu Prapanca in the
*Desawarnana* (*Nagarakrtagama*),
tr. Stuart Robson (Leiden: KITLV
Press, 1995), pp. 38–39 (quoted on
p. 37); a nineteenth-century
impression of Angkor Wat, from
*Le Tour de Monde 2* [1863], p. 299,
cited in Jean-François Jarrige's
Introduction to *Sculpture of Angkor and
Ancient Cambodia: Millennium of Glory*,
ed. by Helen Ibbitson Jessup and
Thierry Zephir (London: Thames
& Hudson, 1997), p. xix (quoted
on p. 41); inscription describing the
piety of Jayavarman VII, cited in
David P. Chandler, *A History of
Cambodia* (Boulder, Colorado:
Westview Press, 1983) p. 61 (quoted
on p. 43); folksong, cited in Li Tana,
*Nguyen Cochinchina: Southern Vietnam
in the Seventeenth and Eighteenth
Centuries* (Ithaca: Cornell University
Southeast Asia Program, 1998), p. 14
(quoted on p. 93); Idrus, *Fujinkai*, in
*Two Stories of the Japanese Occupation*,
tr. by Mrs S.U. Nababan, *Indonesia 2*,
1966, pp. 125–29 (quoted on p. 137).

# INDEX